# THE ULTIMATE

# COCKTAIL

# ENCYCLOPEDIA

IN ASSOCIATION WITH iDRINK.COM

# THE ULTIMATE
# COCKTAIL
## ENCYCLOPEDIA

### WALTER BURNS

THUNDER BAY
P·R·E·S·S

SAN DIEGO

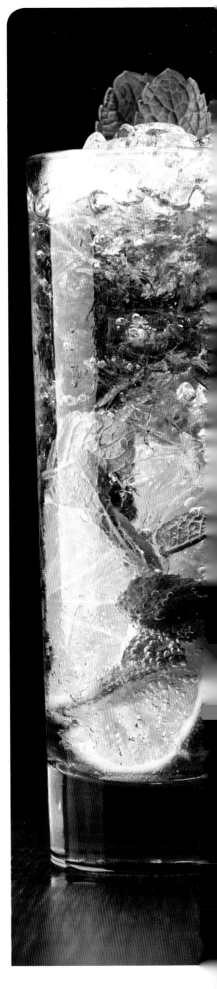

**Thunder Bay Press**
An imprint of the Baker & Taylor Publishing Group
10350 Barnes Canyon Road, San Diego, CA 92121
www.thunderbaybooks.com

Moseley Road Inc, www.moseleyroad.com
Publisher: Sean Moore
General Manager: Karen Prince
Editorial Director: Damien Moore
Art Director: Tina Vaughan
Production Director: Adam Moore

Editorial: Walter Burns
Design: Philippa Baile and Duncan Youel, www.oiloften.co.uk
Photography: Jeremy Baile, Andrew Ridge, Becca MacPhee
at RGB Digital Ltd, www.rgbdigital.co.uk

All notations of errors or omissions should be addressed to
Thunder Bay Press, Editorial Department, at the above address.
All other correspondence (author inquiries, permissions)
concerning the content of this book should be addressed to
Moseley Road Inc., 123 Main St., Irvington, NY 10533, United
States.

The ultimate cocktail encyclopedia / from the editors of iDrink.com.
    pages cm
  Includes bibliographical references and index.
  ISBN-13: 978-1-62686-050-6 (hardback)
  ISBN-10: 1-62686-050-5 (hardback)
  1. Cocktails--Encyclopedias. I. iDrink (Firm)
  TX951.U45 2014
  641.87'4--dc23
    2013038538

Printed in China.
1 2 3 4 5 17 16 15 14 13

# CONTENTS

# C O N T E

# INTRODUCTION

In a sense, cocktails have probably been with us from the start of humanity's long relationship with ethyl alcohol. Archaeologists have found evidence that, even 5,000 years ago, people were brewing alcoholic drinks and experimenting with additives to improve or otherwise modify their flavors. In China, wine has traditionally been drunk with any number of additives, many but not all of them medicinal; in the West, the wine and brandy of the warmer climes and the distilled spirits of the northern regions created lively regional and local traditions.

Over time, those traditions, and the drinks they produced, gained depth, complexity, and variety—not least because, for centuries, drinking water was considered unhealthy (often rightfully, depending on the water source). But the cocktail as we know it is really only a couple of hundred years old. Its more immediate origins probably lie in the shift from fermented to distilled drinks that took place in England in the eighteenth century, with the popularization of gin and "medicinal" drinks derived from grain spirits. From there, it was only a matter of time, curiosity, and experimentation.

## THE ORIGINS OF THE COCKTAIL

The word "cocktail," like many words, has evolved over time, broadening its meaning. While it once indicated a narrow range of drinks—perhaps originally a single drink—it is now customarily used to cover nearly the full range of mixed drinks available in the bars of the world. Purists may insist that a true cocktail include at least three ingredients, two of which are distilled liquor and bitters; others may argue that any drink mixed on the spot from two or more ingredients, at least one of which is alcoholic, is a cocktail. There is no "right" answer here, but for all intents

and purposes we have generally rubbed out the line between cocktails and other mixed drinks.

The first known references to drinks called cocktails come from the late eighteenth and early nineteenth centuries. At that time, alcoholic beverages were largely served in inns and public houses, and weary travelers and thirsty locals would order concoctions such as Toddies, Fizzes, Slings, and Punches— many of which remain available in traditional cocktail bars. Certainly, some kind of drink called a cocktail was being served in London by 1798, when it appeared on the bar tab of no less a personage than William Pitt the Younger. In America, the availability of rum, which had been the most serendipitously popular by-product of the sugar trade, added a new dimension to such drinks. In 1806, one rather drily witty post in a New York publication defined a "cock-tail" as "a stimulating liquor, composed of spirits of any kind, sugar, water, and bitters," and decried its use in getting potential voters drunk and therefore easily swayed on election days.

The word's etymology remains uncertain. Some accounts suggest that its origins lay with using rooster feathers as a garnish. Others point to the French word *coquetier*, a kind of eggcup in which mixed drinks could be served. Still others suggest the colloquial use of the word "cocktail" to refer to a horse whose tail was clipped short to indicate it was a mixed breed—rather like a mixed drink, perhaps. What is certain is that by the middle of the nineteenth century cocktails were big in America. The end of taxes on spirits after the War of 1812, the burgeoning popularity of Bourbon and other American whiskies, and the rise of urban saloons as social and political

# THE RISE, FALL, AND RISE

hubs all contributed to a thriving cocktail culture.

In 1862, Connecticut native Jerry Thomas, who had apparently learned his bartending in London, published *How to Mix Drinks; or, The Bon-Vivant's Companion*, one of many manuals that would appear in the second half of the century. Of the many drink recipes in his book, Thomas only identified ten as cocktails, stipulating that the defining quality of a cocktail is that it contains bitters. Other writers thought differently, but overriding all the disputes was the sheer exuberance and creativity of the cocktail scene, which had become big business. Expert bartenders—known as barmen—were in high demand. As technology improved—ice machines, refrigeration, carbonated water, and the wealth created by industrialization—the quality and variety of drinks increased. This was the era that created the Martini, the Manhattan, the Pousse Café, the Bronx Cocktail, and the Whiskey Sour.

But by 1919, the temperance movement had gradually won its political battle against alcohol, and for the next fourteen years the culture of the cocktail was forced underground. Of course, Prohibition didn't succeed in suppressing the consumption of alcohol; on the contrary, it only provided the perfect arena for organized criminals to reap a handsome profit on the outlaw appetites of thirsty Americans. Speakeasies— secret bars where people gathered to drink and socialize—flourished. Since alcoholic beverages had to be made and transported surreptitiously, the quality of liquor fell off, so a variety of new cocktails were concocted to make the bathtub gin and other inferior spirits more palatable. More importantly, and less happily, the dignity of cocktail culture suffered

a blow from which, arguably, it is only now recovering. The skill and aplomb of the great barmen of the past could no longer be celebrated as it once was, and cocktail bars became associated with organized crime and reckless hedonism. The chastening effect of the Crash in 1929 only made things worse.

In 1933, Prohibition was repealed, and the cocktail came out of hiding. It was no longer the golden age of the cocktail, but it was the Golden Age of Hollywood, and the public delighted to visions of movie stars, onscreen and off, sipping Martinis and Manhattans while exchanging witty dialogue or simply looking gorgeous and stylish. In short, the cocktail had gone from serving as a mainstay of social life to being a prop in collective fantasies of the glamorous life. Some of the best of cocktail culture had survived overseas, in places like the Savoy in London and Harry's American Bar in Paris, but in America the glory days were gone. After the Second World War, cocktails remained popular, but they were gradually cheapened. The influx of vodka—a shift that some purists think of as a disaster—made for drinks where alcohol contributed less and less flavor to the mix. And mixes themselves—that is, the prepared, often artificially flavored cocktail mixes available in powder or liquid form— soon made mixing cocktails no different from mixing frozen fruit juice or powdered Kool-Aid. Cocktails began to seem tacky.

Toward the end of the twentieth century, though, cocktails began to recover their former status as social lubricants and cultural markers. In the 1980s, a new class of young urban professionals—yuppies— found themselves with a good deal of disposable income and a taste for the rare, the expensive, and the sought-

# OF COCKTAIL CULTURE

# THE COCKTAIL REVIVAL

after. At the same time, a countercultural wave gave prominence to the boutique, hand-crafted production over the mass-produced product. The beverage and hospitality industries responded. Craft beers flourished, wine consumers became more knowledgeable, and the single-malt whiskies of Scotland found an appreciative audience. Though the marketing was often absurd, the desire that beverages should have some kind of distinctiveness, some sort of authenticity of origin, some intriguing narrative behind them, was sincere. Even boutique vodkas, tequilas, and gins gained traction in the market.

By the turn of the millennium, this trend had rediscovered the classic cocktail. Hotel bars saw a resurgence of interest, and modern speakeasies and other classic cocktail lounges answered to a kind of nostalgia for a more epicurean, spopisticated culture of drinking. More period movies and television shows — with men in flannel suits and women in waist-cinching outfits sipping traditional libations — tapped into the nostalgia. The cocktail culture that predated "cocktail mixes" and Club Med confections — the established culture of the Martini, the Gimlet, and the Manhattan — stirred anew. And it shows no sign of fading.

## TOOLS AND TECHNIQUES

This book is mostly a compendium of recipes, some classic and some newfangled. But, as any chef will tell you, in the hands of a serious cook a recipe is only a rough guide. Treat these recipes the same way: you can follow them precisely, or trust your palate and make whatever adjustments you see fit. After all, there are, mathematically, an infinite number of possible recipes for a dry martini. That said, there are some basics about mixing drinks to keep in mind.

First, never forget the ice. If a drink calls for ice — and many cocktails are simply shaken with ice and then strained into a glass — you had better use it. Ice is an essential part of most cocktails: it dilutes the alcohol, making the drink not only more approachable and refreshing, but actually more flavorful as well.

Second, mind your ingredients. Use good liquor and fresh juices. Cheap liquor is usually cheap for a reason, so use the best alcoholic beverages you can afford. But don't go too far: using Hine Millesime 1988 Cognac to make a Sidecar isn't sophisticated, it's a foolish and pretentious waste. And unless it specifically states otherwise, wherever a recipe in this book calls for fruit juice, it means fresh fruit juice. It isn't labor intensive to squeeze an orange or lemon, and it makes an enormous difference in the drink.

Third, don't be afraid to do intimidating things like muddling fruit or flaming an orange peel. These are not difficult skills; with a little practice, you can entertain your guests, enjoy yourself, and improve your drinks by creating little cascades of flaming citrus oils when called for, or by mashing up some ingredients in the bottom of a mixing glass, even if it's only with the end of a wooden spoon.

Fourth, don't sweat the glasses too much. Many cocktails are associated with specific glasses — after all, a highball glass is called by that name for a reason. But some of the kinds of glasses listed with recipes here are aspirational, not realistic. If you have a stock of cordial or hurricane glasses, that's great. If not, feel free to improvise. With some tumblers, tall glasses, wine glasses, and cocktail glasses, you'll be fine. Even the cocktail glasses are mostly about presentation.

Fifth, have the necessary hardware. You'll need a good shaker—either a Boston or cobbler shaker is fine, though some might argue otherwise. A well-made jigger with clearly marked measures is essential. One good strainer will do, though having both a coil strainer and a julep strainer might be nice. Have a few long bar spoons and something to muddle with, be it a real muddler or a wooden spoon or pestle. A simple juicer, preferably the manual kind that strains through a sieve into a small cup, should be all you need for fresh juices. Measuring spoons, a small measuring cup, a paring knife, a cutting board, and so forth you can always retrieve from the kitchen, provided you have them.

Finally, a word about shaking. Never mix a drink with a perfunctory shake. All shaken drinks need to be seriously agitated for at least twenty seconds, while some drinks, especially ones with egg in them, need a great deal more. If you're shaking a mixture with ice, your hands should be nearly frozen by the time you strain or pour the drink. And as for shaking versus stirring, when in doubt, shake.

## BEYOND THE RECIPES

It's sometimes said that there are far too many cocktail recipes circulating out there—that we need to rely more on the classics, or at least on the few hundred time-tested recipes that every good bartender ought to know. While there's some merit to that line of thought, I'm all for letting people share what they believe tastes good. Quality has a way of asserting itself, and any new cocktails that deserve wide appreciation may actually get it.

One of the great pleasures of cocktail culture is tinkering behind the bar. Just as you might experiment with how you prepare dinner, feel free to invent cocktails. If you know what you like and have a feel for how flavors and other qualities might combine, you'll likely come up with something you enjoy. One of the more unusual recipes in this book I actually invented with my wife and a friend; if you're interested, I challenge you to figure out which one it is.

I also invite you to keep exploring. Like many things, cocktails only get more fascinating the more you know about them. Get some old cocktail books and bar manuals and test their recipes. Order hard-to-find ingredients from specialty suppliers. Develop a clear sense of your taste. Do you prefer sour or sweet, or a balance of the two? Which classic cocktails do you most enjoy? What variations on the Martini have you found most beguiling? What is your go-to cocktail? If I just want something I know I'll enjoy, I tend to go for a Sidecar—but I'm up for trying almost anything. And I've learned that what seems less than appealing on paper often tastes delicious in the glass.

Lastly, never forget that a key part of cocktail culture is company. Cocktails are meant to be shared, whether that be for celebrations, special events, intimate evenings, or festive gatherings—or just for a relaxing conversation at the end of a long day. In its heyday, cocktail culture also had a civic aspect; it brought people together and kept important conversations alive. So take your cocktails, like all alcoholic beverages, in moderation, and enjoy them in good company. The discoveries will never cease.

# LONG
# DRINKS

LONG DRINKS, ALSO KNOWN AS TALL DRINKS, ARE
SIMPLY DRINKS IN TALL GLASSES WITH LARGER
AMOUNTS OF MIXER THAN SHORT DRINKS. SOME, LIKE
HIGHBALLS, ARE SIMPLE AND STRAIGHTFORWARD;
OTHERS ARE COMPLEX CONCOCTIONS. WHAT THEY
HAVE IN COMMON IS A RELAXED QUALITY, IN THAT
THEY PRESENT A RELATIVELY LOW CONCENTRATION OF
ALCOHOL AND, OFTEN, AN EASY-DRINKING ACCESSIBILITY.

## APPLEJACK COLLINS

2 oz apple brandy

1 oz lemon juice

Club soda

¼ oz simple syrup

4 dashes of bitters

Lemon slice

Combine brandy, lemon juice, bitters, and syrup in a mixing glass and shake with ice. Strain into an ice-filled Collins glass. Fill with club soda, stir, and garnish with lemon slice.

## APRICOT ANISE COLLINS

½ oz apricot brandy

1 ½ oz gin

1 ½ oz anisette

1 oz lemon juice

Club soda

Lemon slice

Combine brandy, gin, anisette, and lemon juice and shake with ice. Strain into an ice-filled Collins glass. Fill with club soda, stir, and garnish with lemon slice.

## B AND B COLLINS

1 ½ oz brandy

½ oz Bénédictine

1 oz lemon juice

1 oz simple syrup

Club soda

Lemon slice

Orange slice

Combine brandy, lemon juice, and syrup and shake with ice. Strain into chilled Collins glass. Fill with club soda and stir. Top with a float of Bénédictine. Garnish with fruit slices.

## BOURBON COLLINS

2 oz bourbon

1 oz lemon juice

½ oz simple syrup

Club soda

Lemon slice

Combine bourbon, lemon juice, and syrup and shake with ice. Strain into an ice-filled Collins glass. Fill with club soda, stir, and garnish with lemon slice.

## BRANDY COLLINS

2 oz brandy

1 oz lemon juice

¼ oz simple syrup

Club soda

Lemon slice

Combine brandy, lemon juice, and syrup and shake with ice. Strain into an ice-filled Collins glass. Fill with club soda, stir, and garnish with lemon slice.

## CUTTY COLLINS

2 oz Cutty Sark brand whisky

1 oz lemon juice

½ oz simple syrup

Club soda

Lemon slice

Combine whisky, lemon juice, and syrup and shake with ice. Strain into an ice-filled Collins glass. Fill with club soda, stir, and garnish with lemon slice.

## GABLES COLLINS

1 ½ oz vodka

1 oz Crème de Noyaux

½ oz lemon juice

½ oz pineapple juice

Club soda

Lemon slice

Pineapple wedge

Combine vodka, Crème de Noyaux, and juices and shake with ice. Strain into an ice-filled Collins glass. Fill with club soda, stir, and garnish with fruit.

## JOCK COLLINS

2 oz Scotch whisky

1 oz lemon juice

½ oz simple syrup

Club soda

Maraschino cherry

Orange slice

Combine whisky, lemon juice, and syrup and shake with ice. Strain into an ice-filled Collins glass. Fill with club soda, stir, and garnish with cherry and orange slice.

## JOE COLLINS

2 oz Scotch whisky

1 oz lemon juice

Cola

Maraschino cherry

Combine whisky and lemon juice and shake with ice. Strain into an ice-filled Collins glass. Fill with cola, stir, and garnish with cherry.

*Bourbon Collins*

## JOHN COLLINS

2 oz bourbon

1 oz lemon juice

½ oz simple syrup

Club soda

Maraschino cherry

Orange slice

Combine bourbon, lemon juice, and syrup and shake with ice. Strain into an ice-filled Collins glass. Fill with club soda, stir, and garnish with cherry and orange slice.

## MINT COLLINS

1 oz mint-flavored gin

1 oz lemon juice

½ oz simple syrup

Club soda

Lemon slice

Mint sprig

Combine gin, lemon juice, and syrup and shake with ice. Strain into an ice-filled Collins glass. Fill with club soda, stir, and garnish with lemon slice and mint sprig.

## SLOE GIN COLLINS

2 oz sloe gin

1 oz lemon juice

Club soda

Lemon slice

Orange slice

Combine sloe gin and lemon juice and shake with ice. Strain into an ice-filled Collins glass. Fill with club soda, stir, and garnish with lemon and orange slices.

## LIME VODKA COLLINS

2 oz lime vodka

1 oz lemon juice

½ oz simple syrup

Club soda

Lime slice

Combine vodka, lemon juice, and syrup and shake with ice. Strain into an ice-filled Collins glass. Fill with club soda, stir, and garnish with lime slice.

## PEDRO COLLINS

2 oz citrus rum

1 oz lime juice

½ oz simple syrup

Club soda

Lemon slice

Maraschino cherry

Combine rum, lime juice, and syrup and shake with ice. Strain into an ice-filled Collins glass. Fill with club soda, stir, and garnish with lemon slice and cherry.

## TEQUILA COLLINS

2 oz tequila

1 oz lemon juice

Club soda

Lime slice

Combine tequila and lemon juice and shake with ice. Strain into an ice-filled Collins glass. Fill with club soda, stir, and garnish with a lime slice.

## MARASCHINO COLLINS

1 ½ oz vodka

1 ½ oz sweet maraschino cherry juice

1 oz lemon juice

Club soda

Maraschino cherry

Lemon slice

Combine vodka, lemon juice, and cherry juice and shake with ice. Strain into an ice-filled Collins glass. Fill with club soda, stir, and garnish with cherry and lemon slice.

## RUM COLLINS

2 oz light rum

1 oz lime juice

½ oz simple syrup

Club soda

Lemon slice

Cherry

Combine rum, lime juice, and syrup and shake with ice. Strain into an ice-filled Collins glass. Fill with club soda, stir, and garnish with lemon slice and cherry.

## TOM COLLINS

1 ½ oz gin

¾ oz lemon juice

1 oz simple syrup

Club soda

Orange slice

Cherry

Combine gin, syrup, and lemon juice and shake with ice. Strain into an ice-filled Collins glass. Fill with club soda, stir, and garnish with cherry and orange slice.

*John Collins*

*Tom Collins*

### VICTORY COLLINS

1 ½ oz vodka

3 oz lemon juice

3 oz unsweetened grape
  juice

½ oz simple syrup

Orange slice

Combine vodka, lemon juice,
grape juice, and syrup and shake
with ice. Strain into an ice-filled
Collins glass and stir. Garnish
with an orange slice.

### VODKA COLLINS

2 oz vodka

1 oz lemon juice

¼ oz simple syrup

Club soda

Lemon slice

Orange slice

Maraschino cherry

Combine vodka, lemon juice, and
syrup and shake with ice. Strain
into an ice-filled Collins glass. Fill
with club soda, stir, and garnish
with lemon and orange slices
and cherry.

### WHISKEY COLLINS

2 oz whiskey of choice

1 oz lemon juice

¼ oz simple syrup

Club soda

Lemon slice

Orange slice

Maraschino cherry

Combine whiskey, lemon juice,
and syrup and shake with ice.
Strain into an ice-filled Collins
glass. Fill with club soda, stir,
and garnish with lemon and
orange slices and cherry.

*Vokda Collins*

*Whiskey Collins*

## APRICOT COOLER

2 oz apricot brandy

Simple syrup

Club soda

Orange peel

In a chilled Collins or highball glass, dissolve a splash of syrup in a small amount of club soda. Fill glass with ice and add brandy. Fill with club soda and stir. Garnish with orange peel.

## BRIDESMAID COOLER

2 oz gin

1 oz lemon juice

¾ oz simple syrup

Dash of Angostura bitters

4 oz ginger ale

Lemon slice

In a chilled Collins or highball glass, combine gin, lemon juice, syrup, and bitters and stir. Fill with ice and then with ginger ale and stir. Garnish with lemon slice.

## CITRONELLA COOLER

1 oz lemon vodka

2 oz lemonade

2 oz cranberry juice

¼ oz lime juice

Lemon wedge

Combine vodka, lemonade, and juices in a Collins glass or other large glass and stir well. Fill with ice and garnish with lemon wedge.

## BOURBON COOLER

2 oz bourbon

4 oz lemon-lime soda

Lemon wedge

In a chilled Collins or highball glass, combine bourbon and soda and stir. Fill with ice, stir again, and garnish with lemon wedge.

## CASTRO COOLER

1 ½ oz gold rum

¾ oz apple brandy

2 oz orange juice

¾ oz lime juice

½ oz lemon juice

Lime slice

Orange slice

Combine all ingredients in a chilled Collins glass or other large glass. Fill with ice and garnish with lime and orange slices.

## COUNTRY CLUB COOLER

2 oz dry vermouth

¼ oz grenadine syrup

Club soda

Orange peel

Lemon peel

In a chilled Collins glass or other large glass, combine grenadine syrup and a small amount of club soda and stir. Add vermouth, fill with club soda, and stir again. Garnish with orange and lemon peels.

## BRANDY COOLER

2 oz brandy

4 oz lemon-lime soda

Lemon wedge

In a chilled Collins or highball glass, combine brandy and soda and stir. Fill with ice, stir again, and garnish with lemon wedge.

## CHARTREUSE COOLER

1 oz Yellow Chartreuse

2 oz orange juice

½ oz lemon juice

3 ½ oz sparkling bitter lemon soda

Orange slice

Lemon slice

Combine Yellow Chartreuse and juices in an ice-filled Collins or other large glass and stir. Fill with bitter lemon soda, stir, and garnish with orange and lemon slices.

## CROCODILE COOLER

1 oz melon liqueur

1 ½ oz vodka

½ oz Cointreau or triple sec

1 oz lemon juice

½ oz simple syrup

Club soda

Lime slice

Combine melon liqueur, vodka, Cointreau, lemon juice, and syrup in a chilled Collins glass or other large glass and stir. Fill with ice and then club soda and stir. Garnish with lime slice.

*Citronella Cooler*

## CURAÇAO COOLER

1 oz triple sec

½ oz vodka

½ oz Blue Curaçao liqueur

½ oz lime juice

½ oz lemon juice

½ oz orange juice

½ oz simple syrup

4 oz lemonade

Lime peel

In a chilled Collins glass or other large glass, combine all ingredients but the lime peel and stir. Fill with ice and garnish with lime peel.

## HARVARD COOLER

2 oz apple brandy

½ oz simple syrup

Club soda

Orange peel

Lemon peel

In a Collins glass or other large glass, dissolve syrup into a small amount of club soda. Fill glass with ice, add apple brandy, and stir. Fill with club soda, stir, and garnish with citrus peels.

## LONE TREE COOLER

2 oz gin

½ oz dry vermouth

½ oz simple syrup

Club soda

Lemon peel

Orange peel

In a Collins glass or other large glass, dissolve syrup into a small amount of club soda. Fill glass with ice, add gin and vermouth, and stir. Fill with club soda, stir, and garnish with citrus peels.

## GIN COOLER

2 oz gin

1 oz simple syrup

Club soda

Orange peel

Lemon peel

In a chilled Collins glass or other large glass, dissolve the simple syrup in a small amount of club soda. Fill glass with ice and add gin. Fill with club soda and stir. Add citrus peels for garnish.

## HONOLULU COOLER

1 ½ oz peach liqueur

2 oz lime juice

Pineapple juice

Lime wedge

In a Collins glass or other large glass, combine peach liqueur and lime juice and stir. Fill with ice, add pineapple juice, and stir. Garnish with lime wedge.

## NORMANDY COOLER

2 oz Calvados

1 oz lemon juice

½ oz simple syrup

¼ oz grenadine syrup

Club soda

Lemon peel

In a Collins glass or other large glass, dissolve syrups into lemon juice and a small amount of club soda. Fill glass with ice, add Calvados, and stir. Fill with club soda, stir, and garnish with lemon peel.

## GORKY PARK COOLER

1 ½ oz strawberry vodka

½ oz spiced rum

½ oz coconut rum

4 oz pineapple juice

Pineapple wedge

Combine vodka, rums, and pineapple juice and shake with ice. Strain into an ice-filled Collins glass or other large glass. Fill with ice and garnish with pineapple wedge.

## KLONDIKE COOLER

2 oz Canadian whisky

½ oz simple syrup

Club soda

Lemon peel

Orange peel

In a Collins glass or other large glass, dissolve syrup into a small amount of club soda. Fill glass with ice, add whisky, and stir. Fill with club soda, stir, and garnish with citrus peels.

## PINEAPPLE COOLER

2 oz dry white wine

2 oz pineapple juice

½ oz simple syrup

Club soda

Lemon peel

Orange peel

In a Collins glass or other large glass, dissolve syrup into the wine, pineapple juice, and a small amount of club soda. Fill glass with ice and club soda, stir, and garnish with citrus peels.

*Curaçao Cooler*

## POLAR BEAR COOLER

2 oz dark rum

1 oz Punt e Mes vermouth

1 oz lemon juice

½ oz orange juice

1 oz simple syrup

Club soda

Lemon peel

Orange peel

In a Collins glass or other large glass, dissolve syrup into a small amount of club soda. Add rum, vermouth, and juices and stir. Fill with ice, top with club soda, stir, and garnish with citrus peels.

## ROCK AND RYE COOLER

1 ½ oz vodka

1 oz Rock and Rye liqueur

½ oz lime juice

½ oz simple syrup

Club soda

Lime peel

In a Collins glass or other large glass, dissolve syrup into a small amount of club soda. Fill glass with ice, add vodka and Rock and Rye, and stir. Fill with club soda, stir, and garnish with lime peel.

## SCOTCH COOLER

2 oz Scotch whisky

White Crème de Menthe

Club soda

In an ice-filled Collins glass or other large glass, combine whisky and Crème de Menthe and stir. Fill with club soda and stir.

## RASPBERRY COOLER

2 oz raspberry vodka

1 oz simple syrup

Club soda

Lemon peel

Lime peel

In a Collins glass or other large glass, dissolve syrup into a small amount of club soda. Fill glass with ice, add vodka, and stir. Top with club soda, stir, and garnish with citrus peels.

## RUM COOLER

2 oz light rum

1 oz lime juice

1 oz simple syrup

Club soda

Lemon wedge

In a Collins glass or other large glass, dissolve syrup into lime juice and a small amount of club soda. Fill glass with ice, add rum, and stir. Fill with club soda, stir, and garnish with lemon wedge.

## SPORRAN COOLER

2 oz Drambuie

1 oz lemon juice

¼ oz grenadine syrup

Angostura bitters

Club soda

Lemon peel

In an ice-filled Collins glass or other large glass, combine Drambuie, lemon juice, grenadine syrup and a dash of bitters, and stir. Fill with club soda, stir, and garnish with lemon peel.

## REMMSEN COOLER

2 oz gin

¾ oz simple syrup

Club soda

Lemon peel

In a Collins glass or other large glass, dissolve syrup into a small amount of club soda. Fill glass with ice, add gin, and stir. Fill with club soda, stir, and garnish with lemon peel.

## SAN JUAN COOLER

2 oz light rum

¾ oz dry vermouth

Pineapple juice

Lime peel

Fill a Collins glass or other large glass with ice. Add rum and vermouth and stir. Fill with pineapple juice, stir, and garnish with lime peel.

## SUMMER COOLER

1 oz vodka

2 oz orange juice

1 oz lime juice

1 oz lemon juice

½ oz simple syrup

Angostura bitters

Club soda

Lemon peel

Orange peel

In a Collins glass or other large glass, dissolve syrup in a small amount of club soda. Add vodka, juices, and two or three dashes of bitters and stir. Fill with ice and then with club soda and stir. Garnish with citrus peels.

*Polar Bear Cooler*

*Tod's Cooler*

## TOD'S COOLER

2 oz gin

⅔ oz Crème de Cassis

⅔ oz lemon juice

Club soda

Lemon peel

In an ice-filled Collins glass or other large glass, combine gin, lemon juice, and Crème de Cassis and stir. Fill with club soda, stir, and garnish with lemon peel.

## TRAFFIC LIGHT COOLER

1 oz gold tequila

¾ oz melon liqueur

½ oz sloe gin

½ oz simple syrup

½ oz lemon juice

2 oz orange juice

Lemon peel

Lime peel

In a Collins glass or other large glass, dissolve syrup in a small amount of club soda. Add melon liqueur, gin, tequila, and juices, and stir. Fill with ice and stir. Garnish with citrus peels.

*Freshly cut limes*

## B'S TROPICAL FIX

2 oz coconut rum

¼ oz Maui Blue Hawaiian schnapps

Cherry cola

Wedge mango

Wedge lime

Shake rum and schnapps with ice. Strain into a highball glass filled with crushed ice, fill with cherry cola, and garnish with mango and lime.

## BRANDY FIX

2 oz brandy

¼ oz simple syrup

¼ oz water

1 oz lemon juice

Maraschino cherry

Lemon slice

Combine the syrup, water, and lemon juice and shake with ice. Strain into a highball glass filled with crushed ice. Add brandy, stir, and garnish with cherry and lemon slice.

## PINK FIX

2 oz gin

¼ oz simple syrup

¾ oz grenadine syrup

2 oz lemon juice

Maraschino cherry

Lemon slice

Combine the syrups and lemon juice and shake with ice. Strain into a highball glass filled with crushed ice. Add gin, stir, and garnish with cherry and lemon slice.

## BAKUNIN

1 ½ oz orange vodka

1 oz Grand Marnier

2 oz orange juice

½ oz lemon juice

Dash of grenadine syrup

Combine all ingredients and shake with ice. Strain into a highball glass filled with crushed ice.

## GIN FIX

2 oz gin

¼ oz simple syrup

¼ oz water

1 oz lemon juice

Maraschino cherry

Lemon slice

Combine the syrup, water, and lemon juice and shake with ice. Strain into a highball glass filled with crushed ice. Add gin, stir, and garnish with cherry and lemon slice.

## QUICK FIX

3 oz Canadian whisky

1 oz cherry whiskey

Lemon-lime soda

Lemon slice

Combine whiskeys and shake with ice. Strain into a highball glass filled with crushed ice. Fill with soda, stir, and garnish with lemon slice.

## BOURBON FIX

2 oz bourbon

¼ oz simple syrup

1 oz lemon juice

Maraschino cherry

Lemon slice

Combine the syrup and lemon juice and shake with ice. Strain into a highball glass filled with crushed ice. Add bourbon, stir, and garnish with cherry and lemon slice.

## IRISH FIX

2 oz Irish whiskey

½ oz Irish Mist liqueur

½ oz lemon juice

1 oz pineapple juice

⅛ oz simple syrup

Lemon slice

Combine all ingredients except the lemon slice and shake with ice. Strain into a highball glass filled with crushed ice. Garnish with lemon slice.

## RUM FIX

2 oz light rum

¼ oz simple syrup

¼ oz water

1 oz lemon juice

Maraschino cherry

Lemon slice

Combine the syrup, water, and lemon juice and shake with ice. Strain into a highball glass filled with crushed ice. Add rum, stir, and garnish with cherry and lemon slice.

*Pink Fix*

### SANTA CRUZ FIX

2 oz Santa Cruz rum
1 oz cherry brandy
½ oz simple syrup
¼ oz water
1 oz lemon juice
Maraschino cherry
Lemon slice

Combine the brandy, syrup, water, and lemon juice and shake with ice. Strain into a highball glass filled with crushed ice. Add rum, stir, and garnish with cherry and lemon slice.

### SCOTCH FIX

2 oz Scotch whisky
¼ oz simple syrup
¼ oz water
1 oz lemon juice
Maraschino cherry
Lemon slice

Combine the syrup, water, and lemon juice and shake with ice. Strain into a highball glass filled with crushed ice. Add whisky, stir, and garnish with cherry and lemon slice.

### WHISKEY FIX

2 oz whiskey of choice
¼ oz simple syrup
¼ oz water
1 oz lemon juice
Maraschino cherry
Lemon slice

Combine the syrup, water, and lemon juice and shake with ice. Strain into a highball glass filled with crushed ice. Add whiskey, stir, and garnish with cherry and lemon slice.

*Scotch Fix*

*Whiskey Fix*

## ALABAMA FIZZ

1 ½ oz gin

¾ oz lemon juice

1 oz simple syrup

Club soda

2 sprigs mint

Combine the gin, lemon juice, and syrup and shake with ice. Strain into a Collins glass filled with ice. Fill with club soda, stir, and garnish with mint sprigs.

## APRICOT ORANGE FIZZ

4 oz light rum

2 oz apricot brandy

12 oz orange juice

2 oz lime juice

Club soda

Lime slice

Combine all ingredients except soda and lime slice, stir, and pour into Collins glasses filled with ice. Top with club soda. Garnish with lime slice.

## BIRD OF PARADISE FIZZ

1 ½ oz gin

½ oz blackberry brandy

¾ oz lemon juice

1 oz simple syrup

1 egg white

Club soda

Combine the gin, brandy, lemon juice, egg white, and syrup and shake with ice. Strain into a chilled Collins glass. Fill with club soda and stir.

## ALBEMARLE FIZZ

1 ½ oz gin

¾ oz lemon juice

1 oz raspberry syrup

Club soda

Combine the gin, lemon juice, and syrup and shake with ice. Strain into a Collins glass filled with ice. Fill with club soda and stir.

## BARCELONA FIZZ

1 ½ oz sweet sherry

1 oz gin

1 oz lemon juice

1 oz simple syrup

Club soda

Combine the sherry, gin, lemon juice, and syrup and shake with ice. Strain into a Collins glass filled with ice. Fill with club soda and stir.

## BLACKBERRY FIZZ

1 ½ oz blackberry brandy

1 ½ oz orange juice

1 oz lemon juice

¼ oz simple syrup

Club soda

Combine the brandy, juices, and syrup and shake with ice. Strain into a Collins glass filled with ice. Fill with club soda and stir.

## APPLE BLOW FIZZ

1 ½ oz apple brandy

¾ oz lemon juice

1 oz simple syrup

1 egg white

Club soda

Combine the brandy, lemon juice, egg white, and syrup and shake with ice. Strain into a chilled Collins glass. Fill with club soda and stir.

## BAYARD FIZZ

1 ½ oz gin

½ oz maraschino liqueur

1 oz lime juice

¼ oz raspberry syrup

Club soda

Raspberry

Combine gin, maraschino liqueur, lime juice, and syrup and shake with ice. Strain into a Collins glass filled with ice. Fill with club soda, stir, and garnish with raspberry.

## BRANDY FIZZ

1 ½ oz brandy

¾ oz lemon juice

1 oz simple syrup

Club soda

Combine the brandy, lemon juice, and syrup and shake with ice. Strain into a Collins glass filled with ice. Fill with club soda and stir.

Albemarle Fizz

## CHERRY FIZZ

1 ½ oz cherry brandy
¾ oz lemon juice
1 oz simple syrup
Club soda

Combine the brandy, lemon juice, and syrup and shake with ice. Strain into a Collins glass filled with ice. Fill with club soda and stir.

## DIAMOND FIZZ

1 ½ oz gin
¾ oz lemon juice
1 oz simple syrup
Brut champagne

Combine the gin, lemon juice, and syrup and shake with ice. Strain into a Collins glass filled with ice. Fill with champagne and stir.

## GIN CASSIS FIZZ

1 ½ oz gin
¾ oz lemon juice
¾ oz simple syrup
Club soda
½ oz Crème de Cassis

Combine the gin, lemon juice, and syrup and shake with ice. Strain into a Collins glass filled with ice. Fill with club soda, stir, and top with Crème de Cassis.

## CHICAGO FIZZ

1 oz light rum
1 oz port
1 oz lemon juice
½ oz simple syrup
1 egg white
Club soda

Combine the rum, port, lemon juice, egg white, and syrup and shake with ice. Strain into a chilled Collins glass. Fill with club soda and stir.

## DUBONNET FIZZ

2 oz Dubonnet
¼ oz cherry brandy
1 oz orange juice
½ oz lemon juice
¼ oz simple syrup
Club soda

Combine the Dubonnet, brandy, juices, and syrup and shake with ice. Strain into a Collins glass filled with ice. Fill with club soda and stir.

## GIN FIZZ

1 ½  oz gin
¾ oz lemon juice
1 oz simple syrup
Club soda

Combine the gin, lemon juice, and syrup and shake with ice. Strain into a Collins glass filled with ice. Fill with club soda and stir.

## DERBY FIZZ

1 oz Scotch whisky
½ oz triple sec
¾ oz lemon juice
½ oz simple syrup
1 egg white
Club soda

Combine the whisky, triple sec, lemon juice, egg white, and syrup and shake with ice. Strain into a chilled Collins glass. Fill with club soda and stir.

## EDITH'S FIZZ

1 ½ oz Lillet Blanc
½ oz maraschino liqueur
4 oz orange juice
Club soda

Combine the Lillet, liqueur, and orange juice and shake with ice. Strain into a Collins glass filled with ice. Fill with club soda and stir.

## GOLDEN FIZZ

1 ½ oz gin
¾ oz lemon juice
1 ½ oz simple syrup
1 oz egg, beaten
Club soda

Combine the gin, lemon juice, egg, and syrup and shake with ice. Strain into a chilled Collins glass. Fill with club soda and stir.

Gin Fizz

Gin Fizz

## GOLDEN RYE FIZZ

1 ½ oz rye whiskey
¼ oz Advocaat liqueur
¼ oz orange juice
1 oz lemon juice
¼ oz simple syrup
Club soda
Maraschino cherry

Combine the rye, liqueur, juices, and syrup and shake with ice. Strain into a Collins glass filled with ice. Fill with club soda, stir, and garnish with cherry.

## IMPERIAL FIZZ

1 oz whiskey
½ oz light rum
¾ oz lemon juice
1 oz simple syrup
Club soda

Combine the whiskey, rum, lemon juice, and syrup and shake with ice. Strain into a Collins glass filled with ice. Fill with club soda and stir.

## MANILA FIZZ

1 ½ oz gin
¾ oz lemon juice
½ oz simple syrup
1 oz egg, beaten
Root beer

Combine the gin, lemon juice, egg, and syrup and shake with ice. Strain into a chilled Collins glass. Fill with root beer and stir.

## GREEN FIZZ

1 ½ oz gin
¼ oz crème de menthe
¾ oz lemon juice
¾ oz simple syrup
1 egg white
Club soda

Combine the gin, crème de menthe, lemon juice, egg white, and syrup and shake with ice. Strain into a chilled Collins glass. Fill with club soda and stir.

## JAMAICAN FIZZ

2 ½ oz dark rum
1 ½ oz pineapple juice
¾ oz simple syrup
Club soda
Lemon slice

Combine the rum, pineapple juice, and syrup and shake with ice. Strain into a Collins glass filled with ice. Fill with club soda, stir, and garnish with lemon slice.

## MAY BLOSSOM FIZZ

2 oz Swedish punsch
¾ oz lemon juice
1 oz grenadine syrup
Club soda

Combine the punsch, lemon juice, and syrup and shake with ice. Strain into a Collins glass filled with ice. Fill with club soda and stir.

## HONG KONG FIZZ

½ oz vodka
½ oz gin
½ oz Bénédictine
½ oz Yellow Chartreuse
1 oz lemon juice
1 oz simple syrup
Club soda

Combine the vodka, gin, liqueurs, lemon juice, and syrup and shake with ice. Strain into a Collins glass filled with ice. Fill with club soda and stir.

## JAPANESE FIZZ

1 ½ oz gin
¾ oz lemon juice
¾ oz simple syrup
½ oz ruby port
1 egg white
Club soda

Combine the gin, port, lemon juice, egg white, and syrup and shake with ice. Strain into a chilled Collins glass. Fill with club soda and stir.

## MERRY WIDOW FIZZ

1 ½ oz sloe gin
¾ oz lemon juice
¾ oz orange juice
1 oz simple syrup
1 egg white
Club soda

Combine the gin, juices, egg white, and syrup and shake with ice. Strain into a chilled Collins glass. Fill with club soda and stir.

*Merry Widow Fizz*

## MORNING GLORY FIZZ

1 ½ oz Scotch whisky

¾ oz lemon juice

1 oz simple syrup

½ oz egg white

Dash of Angostura bitters

Club soda

Combine the whisky, lemon juice, bitters, egg white, and syrup and shake with ice. Strain into a chilled Collins glass. Fill with club soda and stir.

## ROOT BEER FIZZ

1 ½ oz gin

1 oz lemon juice

½ oz simple syrup

Root beer

Combine the gin, lemon juice, and syrup and shake with ice. Strain into a Collins glass filled with ice. Fill with root beer and stir.

## ROYALTY FIZZ

1 ½ oz gin

¾ oz lemon juice

1 oz simple syrup

1 egg, beaten

¼ oz Blue Curaçao

Club soda

Combine the gin, lemon juice, egg, and syrup and shake with ice. Strain into a chilled Collins glass. Fill with club soda and stir. Top with Blue Curaçao.

## PINK FIZZY

1 ½ oz watermelon schnapps

¾ oz lemon juice

1 oz simple syrup

Club soda

Combine the schnapps, lemon juice, and syrup and shake with ice. Strain into a Collins glass filled with ice. Fill with club soda and stir.

## ROYAL FIZZ

1 ½ oz gin

¾ oz lemon juice

1 oz simple syrup

1 egg, beaten

¼ oz Chambord

Club soda

Combine the gin, lemon juice, egg, and syrup and shake with ice. Strain into a chilled Collins glass. Fill with club soda and stir. Top with Chambord.

## RUBY FIZZ

1 ½ oz sloe gin

¾ oz lemon juice

½ oz grenadine syrup

¾ oz simple syrup

1 egg white

Club soda

Combine the gin, lemon juice, egg white, and syrups and shake with ice. Strain into a chilled Collins glass. Fill with club soda and stir.

## RAMOS FIZZ

1 ½ oz gin

½ oz lemon juice

½ oz lime juice

1 ¼ oz simple syrup

2 oz milk

1 egg white

2 drops orange-flower water

Club soda

Combine the gin, juices, milk, egg white, orange-flower water, and syrup and shake with ice. Strain into a chilled Collins glass. Fill with club soda and stir.

## ROYAL GIN FIZZ

1 ½ oz gin

¾ oz lemon juice

1 oz simple syrup

¼ oz Chambord

Club soda

Combine the gin, lemon juice, and syrup and shake with ice. Strain into a Collins glass filled with ice. Fill with club soda and stir. Top with Chambord.

## RUM FIZZ

1 ½ oz white rum

¾ oz lemon juice

1 oz simple syrup

Club soda

Combine the rum, lemon juice, and syrup and shake with ice. Strain into a Collins glass filled with ice. Fill with club soda and stir.

*Royalty Fizz*

**Whiskey Fizz**

## SEA FIZZ

1 ½ oz absinthe
¾ oz lemon juice
1 oz simple syrup
1 egg white
Club soda

Combine the absinthe, lemon juice, egg white, and syrup and shake with ice. Strain into a chilled Collins glass. Fill with club soda and stir.

## SLOE GIN FIZZ

1 ½ oz sloe gin
¾ oz lemon juice
1 oz simple syrup
Club soda

Combine the gin, lemon juice, and syrup and shake with ice. Strain into a Collins glass filled with ice. Fill with club soda and stir.

## TROPICAL PEAR FIZZ

1 oz white rum
½ oz pear liqueur
½ oz banana liqueur
¾ oz lemon juice
½ oz simple syrup
Club soda

Combine the rum, liqueurs, lemon juice, and syrup and shake with ice. Strain into a Collins glass filled with ice. Fill with club soda and stir.

## SILVER FIZZ

1 ½ oz gin
¾ oz lemon juice
1 ½ oz simple syrup
1 egg white
Club soda

Combine the gin, lemon juice, egg white, and syrup and shake with ice. Strain into a Collins glass filled with ice. Fill with club soda and stir.

## TEQUILA FIZZ

1 ½ oz tequila
¾ oz lemon juice
1 oz simple syrup
Club soda

Combine the tequila, lemon juice, and syrup and shake with ice. Strain into a Collins glass filled with ice. Fill with club soda and stir.

## VODKA FIZZ

1 ½ oz vodka
¾ oz lemon juice
1 oz simple syrup
Club soda

Combine the vodka, lemon juice, and syrup and shake with ice. Strain into a Collins glass filled with ice. Fill with club soda and stir.

*Selection of many types of whiskey*

## WHISKEY FIZZ

1 ½ oz whiskey
¾ oz lemon juice
1 ½ oz simple syrup
Dash of Angostura bitters
Club soda

Combine the whiskey, lemon juice, bitters, and syrup and shake with ice. Strain into a Collins glass filled with ice. Fill with club soda and stir.

## BLACKBERRY JULEP

2 oz crème de mure

1 oz orange juice

½ oz simple syrup

½ oz mixed berry marinade

2 sprigs mint

Muddle one mint sprig with the syrup in the bottom of a highball glass and fill with crushed ice. Combine crème de mure and juice and shake with ice. Strain into the highball glass. Top with berry marinade and garnish with mint sprig.

## JOCOSE JULEP

1 ½ oz bourbon

½ oz green crème de menthe

1 oz simple syrup

1 oz lime juice

2 sprigs mint

Muddle one mint sprig with the syrup in the bottom of a highball glass and fill with crushed ice. Combine bourbon, crème de menthe, and lime juice and shake with ice. Strain into the highball glass. Garnish with mint sprig.

## PEACH BRANDY JULEP

2 oz Cognac

½ oz peach brandy

2 peach wedges

2 sprigs mint

Muddle one mint sprig with the peach wedges and peach brandy in the bottom of a mixing glass. Add Cognac and shake. Strain into a highball glass filled with crushed ice. Garnish with mint sprig.

## DIXIE JULEP

2 oz bourbon

¼ oz Southern Comfort

½ oz simple syrup

2 sprigs mint

Muddle one mint sprig with the syrup in the bottom of a highball glass and fill with crushed ice. Combine bourbon and Southern Comfort and shake with ice. Strain into the highball glass. Garnish with mint sprig.

## MARRYAT'S MINT JULEP

1 oz brandy

1 oz peach brandy

¾ oz simple syrup

2 sprigs mint

Muddle one mint sprig with the syrup in the bottom of a highball glass and fill with crushed ice. Combine brandy and peach brandy and shake with ice. Strain into the highball glass. Garnish with mint sprig.

## PINEAPPLE JULEP

2 oz bourbon

1 oz simple syrup

3 wedges pineapple

Several mint leaves

2 sprigs mint

Muddle the mint leaves with the pineapple wedges and syrup in the bottom of a mixing glass. Add bourbon and shake with ice. Strain into a highball glass filled with crushed ice. Garnish with mint sprigs.

## GEORGIA MINT JULEP

1 ½ oz brandy

½ oz peach brandy

½ oz simple syrup

2 sprigs mint

Muddle one mint sprig with the syrup in the bottom of a highball glass and fill with crushed ice. Combine brandy and peach brandy and shake with ice. Strain into the highball glass. Garnish with mint sprig.

## MINT JULEP

2 oz bourbon

½ oz simple syrup

2 sprigs mint

Muddle one mint sprig with the syrup in the bottom of a highball glass and fill with crushed ice. Add bourbon. Garnish with mint sprig.

## RAINBOW JULEP

2 oz bourbon

½ oz apricot brandy

2 sprigs mint

Muddle one mint sprig with the apricot brandy in the bottom of a mixing glass. Add bourbon and shake with ice. Strain into a highball glass filled with crushed ice. Garnish with mint sprig.

*Mint Julep*

## BOMBAY PUNCH

16 oz sweet sherry

16 oz brandy

3 oz triple sec

3 oz maraschino liqueur

2 750ml bottles champagne

1 liter club soda

6 oz simple syrup

Combine ingredients in punch bowl over a block or ring of ice and stir. Garnish with fruits.

## CAPE CODDER PUNCH

3 32oz bottles cranberry-apple drink

24 oz vodka

16 oz orange juice

6 oz lemon juice

6 oz simple syrup

1 28oz bottle mineral water

Combine ingredients in a punch bowl over a block or ring of ice and stir. Garnish with fruits.

## CHAMPAGNE SHERBET PUNCH

1 750ml bottle champagne

24 oz pineapple juice

2 oz lemon juice

1 qt pineapple sherbet

Combine juices in a punch bowl over a block or ring of ice. Just before serving, scoop the sherbet into the bowl and add champagne. Garnish with fruits.

## BOOM BOOM PUNCH

1 750ml bottle of champagne

1 750ml bottle of sweet vermouth

64 oz light rum

32 oz orange juice

Combine ingredients in a punch bowl over a block or ring of ice and stir. Garnish with fruits.

## CARDINAL PUNCH

12 oz lemon juice

16 oz brandy

16 oz light rum

7 oz champagne

64 oz red wine

8 oz sweet vermouth

32 oz club soda

Simple syrup to taste

Combine syrup and lemon juice until sweet to taste. Then combine all ingredients in a punch bowl over a block or ring of ice and stir. Garnish with fruits.

## CHOCOLATE PUNCH

2 oz cognac

1 oz ruby port

1 oz dark crème de cacao

1 oz simple syrup

2 oz heavy cream

Nutmeg

Combine all ingredients but nutmeg and shake with ice. Strain into a chilled old-fashioned glass. Dust with nutmeg.

## BRANDY PUNCH

16 oz brandy

4 oz dark rum

1 oz lemon juice

8 oz water

12 oz ginger ale

Combine all ingredients in a punch bowl over a block or ring of ice and stir. Garnish with fruits.

## CHAMPAGNE PUNCH

2 750ml bottles champagne

16 oz brandy

8 oz triple sec

8 oz maraschino liqueur

16 oz club soda

24 oz lemon juice

Simple syrup to taste

Combine syrup and lemon juice until sweet to taste. Then combine all ingredients in a punch bowl over a block or ring of ice and stir. Garnish with fruits.

## CIDER CUP

2 oz brandy

1 oz triple sec

1 oz simple syrup

6 oz club soda

16 oz apple cider

Fill a large glass pitcher with ice. Combine all the ingredients and stir. Serve in red wine glasses, garnishing with fruits.

*Bombay Punch*

## CIDER NECTAR

2 oz Calvados

4 oz medium sherry

2 oz simple syrup

2 oz pineapple syrup

1 quart apple cider

8 oz club soda

1 lemon, quartered

1 sprig lemon verbena

Nutmeg

Muddle the lemon verbena, lemon, and syrups. Add the remaining ingredients apart from the soda and nutmeg and chill. Add soda just before serving, with ice. Dust with nutmeg.

## COCO'S PUNCH

¾ oz light rum

¾ oz añejo rum

½ oz dark rum

¼ oz coconut rum

2 oz orange juice

3 oz pineapple juice

Splash of grenadine

Dash of Angostura bitters

Maraschino cherry

Orange slice

Combine the rums, juices, grenadine, and bitters and shake with ice. Strain into a large goblet or other specialty glass. Garnish with orange slice and cherry.

## GLOGG

4 oz vodka

1 750ml bottle red wine

Sugar

Raisins

Blanched almond slices

5 crushed cardamom pods

5 whole cloves

1 cinnamon stick

1 orange peel

Set aside some raisins and almonds. Combine wine, raisins, almonds, peel, and spices in a sealed container. Let stand for 24 hours, then heat the mixture and add the vodka, with sugar to taste. Garnish with raisins and almonds.

## CLARET CUP

2 oz brandy

1 oz triple sec

16 oz red wine

2 oz simple syrup

6 oz club soda

Fill a large glass pitcher with ice. Combine all ingredients and stir. Garnish with fruits.

## EGG NOG

6 eggs, separated

¾ cup sugar

1 quart milk

1 pint cream

6 oz bourbon

6 oz spiced rum

Nutmeg

Beat the egg yolks well, adding ½ cup of the sugar while doing so. Add the milk, cream, and liquor. Then beat the egg whites with the remaining sugar until they peak. Fold the egg whites into the mixture. Sprinkle with fresh nutmeg.

## GREEN TEA PUNCH

4 oz brandy

4 oz rum

2 oz curaçao

16 oz hot green tea

9 ounces guava jelly

Juice and peels of two
lemons

Lemon verbena leaf

Dissolve the jelly in the hot tea and stir in the rest of the ingredients. Serve hot, garnished with verbena leaf.

## CLARET PUNCH

16 oz brandy

8 oz triple sec

3 750ml bottles red wine

24 oz lemon juice

Simple syrup

32 oz club soda

Add syrup to lemon juice until sweet to taste. Pour into punch bowl over block or ring of ice. Add other ingredients and stir. Garnish with fruits.

## FISH HOUSE PUNCH

16 oz light rum

32 oz peach brandy

48 oz brandy

24 oz lemon juice

Simple syrup

32 oz club soda

Add syrup to lemon juice until sweet to taste. Pour into punch bowl over a block or ring of ice. Add other ingredients and stir. Garnish with fruits.

## HOT APPLE BRANDY

12 oz apricot brandy

48 oz apple juice

3 cinnamon sticks

½ tsp ground cloves

Combine all ingredients and simmer over low heat for half an hour. Serve hot in mugs or brandy snifters.

*Egg Nog*

## HOT RUMMED CIDER

12 oz light rum
1 ½ qts apple cider
6 tbsp brown sugar
3 tbsp butter

Bring cider and brown sugar to boil in a saucepan. Reduce heat and melt in butter. Add rum and serve hot in mugs.

## KENTUCKY PUNCH

32 oz bourbon
12 oz frozen orange juice concentrate, thawed
12 oz frozen lemonade concentrate, thawed
8 oz lemon juice
1 2-liter bottle lemon-lime soda

Combine all ingredients but the soda in a pitcher and chill. Pour into a punch bowl over a block or ring of ice and stir in soda. Garnish with fruits.

## PICON PUNCH

2 oz Amer Picon
½ oz lemon juice
½ oz grenadine syrup
Club soda or ginger ale

Combine Amer Picon, lemon juice, and syrup and shake well with ice. Strain into a highball glass filled with ice. Top with soda or ginger ale. Garnish with fruits.

## HOT SPICED CIDER

1 gallon apple cider
Calvados
8 cinnamon sticks
6 star anise
10 cloves
10 allspice berries, cracked

In a stockpot, combine all ingredients except Calvados and simmer slowly for at least two hours. Pour one ounce of Calvados in each mug and fill with cider (or drink without alcohol).

## LOVING CUP

2 oz brandy
1 oz triple sec
16 oz red wine
1 oz simple syrup
6 oz club soda

Fill a large glass pitcher with ice and stir in all the ingredients. Garnish with fruits.

## PILGRIM COCKTAIL

½ oz dark rum
½ oz light rum
½ oz orange curaçao
2 oz orange juice
¾ oz lime juice
¼ oz pimento liqueur
Dash of Angostura bitters

Combine all ingredients, shake with ice, and strain into a chilled cocktail or old-fashioned glass.

## INDEPENDENCE DAY PUNCH (NON-ALCOHOLIC)

4 oz chilled black tea
1 ½ oz simple syrup
¾ oz lemon juice
4 oz watermelon balls
Lemon wheel for garnish

In the bottom of a mixing glass, muddle the watermelon with the simple syrup. Add the lemon juice and black tea and shake with ice. Strain into a goblet or Collins glass filled with ice and garnish with lemon.

## MINT JULEP PUNCH

24 oz bourbon
48 oz pineapple juice
6 oz lime juice
16 oz water
10 oz mint jelly
56 oz lemon-lime soda
Mint sprigs

In a saucepan, melt jelly into water, stirring over low heat, and let cool. Combine with bourbon and juices in a glass pitcher and chill. When ready to serve, stir in soda. Serve in Collins glasses, garnished with mint sprigs.

## PIMM'S PUNCH

8 oz Pimm's No. 1
32 oz lemon-lime soda
Cucumber
Mixed fruits (apple, orange, lemon, etc.)

Combine Pimm's, soda, and mixed fruits in a glass pitcher over ice. Serve garnished with slivers of cucumber.

*Hot Spiced Cider*

## PLANTER'S PUNCH

5 oz dark rum

5 oz light rum

3 oz orange curaçao

12 oz orange juice

12 oz pineapple juice

4 oz lime juice

4 oz grenadine

½ oz Angostura bitters

Mixed fruits (orange, lime, pineapple)

Combine all ingredients except fruits in a large glass pitcher and stir well. Serve over ice and garnish with mixed fruit.

## PORT WHISKEY PUNCH

1 ½ oz bourbon

1 oz ruby port

¾ oz lemon juice

1 ½ oz orange juice

1 ½ oz cranberry juice

1 oz simple syrup

Orange slice

Combine whiskey, juices, and syrup and shake with ice. Strain into a highball glass filled with ice and top with the port. Garnish with orange slice.

## SANGRIA

1 750ml bottle Spanish red wine

3 oz orange curaçao

2 oz lemon juice

2 oz simple syrup

3 oz orange juice

3 oz white grape juice

Club soda

Orange, lemon, and lime wheels

In the bottom of a glass pitcher, muddle the fruit wheels with the lemon juice and syrup. Add the juices, wine, and curaçao and stir. Top with club soda and serve over ice in red wine glasses. Garnish with fresh fruit if desired.

## SMUGGLERS' BREW

12 oz dark rum

4 oz brandy

32 oz black tea

3 tbsp butter

½ cup sugar

½ tsp nutmeg

In a large saucepan, combine all ingredients except the brandy and bring slowly to a boil. Warm the brandy separately and add to the mixture. Serve in mugs or Irish coffee glasses.

## TI PUNCH

1 ½ oz rum

½ oz Falernum syrup

½ oz simple syrup

¾ oz lime juice

Lime wedge

Combine all ingredients except the lime wedge and shake with ice. Strain into a chilled old-fashioned glass and garnish with a squeezed lime wedge.

*White grapes*

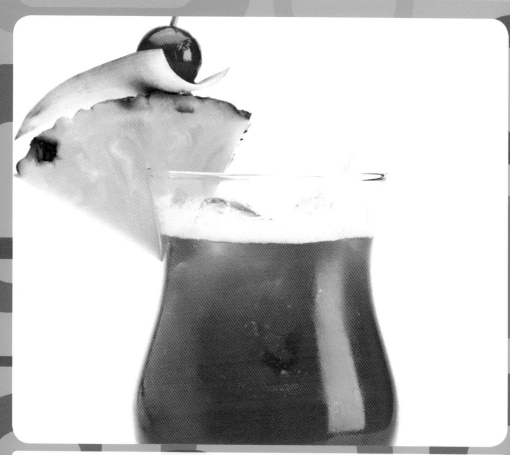

Planter's Punch

Sangria

## TOM AND JERRY

*Batter:*

12 eggs, separated

3 pounds sugar

2 tsp ground cinnamon

½ tsp ground cloves

½ tsp ground allspice

2 oz dark rum

In a large bowl, beat the egg yolks until very thin, adding the sugar in the process. Separately, beat the egg whites until stiff. Add the rum and spices to the yolks and mix in the whites.

*Drink:*

2 tbsp batter

1 ½ oz brandy

½ oz dark rum

4 oz boiling water

Nutmeg

Spoon the batter into the bottom of a mug. Add the spirits and boiling water and stir. Dust with nutmeg.

## WEST INDIAN PUNCH

64 oz light rum

1 750ml bottle crème de banane

32 oz pineapple juice

32 oz orange juice

32 oz lemon juice

6 oz simple syrup

1 tsp ground nutmeg

½ tsp ground clove

1 tsp cinnamon

6 oz club soda

Stir syrup and spices into club soda and pour into a large punch bowl over a block or ring of ice. Add remaining ingredients and stir. Garnish with fresh fruit.

## WHISKEY SOUR PUNCH

32 oz bourbon

24 oz orange juice

3 cans frozen lemonade concentrate

1 2-liter bottle club soda

Combine all ingredients in a punch bowl with a block or ring of ice. Garnish with fresh fruit.

## WHITE WINE CUP

16 oz white wine

2 oz brandy

½ oz triple sec

½ oz Curaçao

1 oz simple syrup

6 oz club soda

Combine all ingredients in a glass pitcher with ice and stir. Garnish with fresh fruit and serve in white wine glasses.

## WINTER PUNCH

1 gallon apple cider

12 oz rum

8 oz peach brandy

6 oz peach schnapps

6 cinnamon sticks

In a saucepan, bring cider and cinnamon to a rolling boil. Reduce heat and add rum, brandy, and schnapps. Stir until piping hot. Serve in mugs or coffee glasses.

*Dried cinnamon sticks*

*White Wine Cup*

# CLASSIC COCKTAILS

Some drinks have become timeless, iconic libations of cocktail culture:

## THE MARTINI

Despite a myriad of variations since its first appearance in the nineteenth century, the classic Martini remains the quintessential elegant cocktail: a cool, somewhat austere drink, not showy, but certainly powerful.

## THE MANHATTAN

The richness and power of whiskey gives the Manhattan slightly rougher edges than the Martini. It gained prominence in the 1930s as one of the five Borough cocktails of New York.

## THE OLD FASHIONED

Long before Don Draper of *Mad Men* revived interest in this classic, adding bitters and sugar to whiskey was a mainstay of cocktail culture and one of the most basic drink preparations.

## THE DAIQUIRI

The classic rum cocktail, the Daiquiri was a favorite of Ernest Hemingway and John F. Kennedy, and has spawned a host of variations.

Old Fashioned

Strawberry Daiquiri

Cutty Rickey

## APPLE BRANDY RICKEY

1 ½ oz apple brandy

½ oz lime juice

5 oz club soda

Lime slice

Combine brandy and lime juice in an ice-filled highball glass. Add soda and stir. Garnish with lime slice.

## APRICOT BRANDY RICKEY

1 ½ oz apricot brandy

½ oz lime juice

5 oz club soda

Lime slice

Combine brandy and lime juice in an ice-filled highball glass. Add soda and stir. Garnish with lime slice.

## CUTTY RICKEY

1 ½ oz Cutty Sark Scotch whisky

½ oz lime juice

5 oz club soda

Lime slice

Combine whisky and lime juice in an ice-filled highball glass. Add soda and stir. Garnish with lime slice.

## APPLE RUM RICKEY

¾ oz apple brandy

¾ oz light rum

½ oz lime juice

5 oz club soda

Lime slice

Combine brandy, rum, and lime juice in an ice-filled highball glass. Add soda and stir. Garnish with lime slice.

## BRANDY RICKEY

1 ½ oz brandy

½ oz lime juice

5 oz club soda

Lime slice

Combine brandy and lime juice in an ice-filled highball glass. Add soda and stir. Garnish with lime slice.

## GIN LIME RICKEY

1 ½ oz gin

½ oz lime juice

Club soda

2 lime wedges

In the bottom of a highball glass, muddle one lime wedge with a small amount of soda. Fill glass with ice nearly to the top and add gin and lime juice. Fill with soda and stir. Garnish with lime wedge.

## APPLEJACK RUM RICKEY

1 oz apple brandy

½ oz gold rum

½ oz lime juice

5 oz club soda

Lime slice

Combine brandy, rum, and lime juice in an ice-filled highball glass. Add soda and stir. Garnish with lime slice.

## CITY RICKEY

1 ½ oz gin

1 oz Cointreau or triple sec

½ oz lime juice

1 ½ oz cranberry juice

Club soda

Lime slice

Combine gin, Cointreau, and lime juice in an ice-filled highball glass. Fill with soda and cranberry juice and stir. Garnish with lime slice.

## GIN RICKEY

1 ½ oz gin

½ oz lime juice

5 oz club soda

Lime slice

Combine gin and lime juice over ice in a highball glass. Add soda and stir. Garnish with lime slice.

## GRAPE JUICE RICKEY

1 ½ oz gin

1 oz red grape juice

½ oz lime juice

2 oz club soda

Lime slice

Combine gin and juices in an ice-filled highball glass. Add soda and stir. Garnish with lime slice.

## LIME RICKEY (NON-ALCOHOLIC)

¾ oz lime juice

1 oz simple syrup

3 dashes of Angostura bitters

Club soda

Lime peel

Combine lime juice, syrup, and bitters in an ice-filled Collins glass. Top with soda and stir. Garnish with lime peel.

## RUM RICKEY

1 ½ oz white rum

½ oz lime juice

5 oz club soda

Lime slice

Combine rum and lime juice over ice in a highball glass. Add soda and stir. Garnish with lime slice.

## GRAPE RICKEY

1 ½ oz grape vodka

½ oz lime juice

5 oz club soda

Lime slice

Combine vodka and lime juice over ice in a highball glass. Add soda and stir. Garnish with lime slice.

## RUMLESS RICKEY (NON-ALCOHOLIC)

1 oz lime juice

¼ oz grenadine syrup

Dash of Angostura bitters

6 oz club soda

Lime slice

Combine lime juice, grenadine, and bitters in an ice-filled old-fashioned glass. Top with soda and stir. Garnish with lime slice.

## SCOTCH RICKEY

1 ½ oz single-malt Scotch whisky

½ oz lime juice

5 oz club soda

Lime slice

Combine whisky and lime juice over ice in a highball glass. Add soda and stir. Garnish with lime slice.

## IRISH RICKEY

1 ½ oz Irish whiskey

½ oz lime juice

5 oz club soda

Lime slice

Combine whiskey and lime juice over ice in a highball glass. Add soda and stir. Garnish with lime slice.

*Freshly sliced lime*

*Grape Juice Rickey*

### SLOE GIN RICKEY

1 ½ oz sloe gin
½ oz lime juice
5 oz club soda
Lime slice

Combine gin and lime juice over ice in a highball glass. Add soda and stir. Garnish with lime slice.

### STONE RICKEY

1 ½ oz gin
½ oz lime juice
2 oz orange juice
1 oz simple syrup
3 oz club soda
Orange slice

Combine gin, juices, and syrup in a highball glass nearly filled with ice. Add soda and stir. Garnish with orange slice.

### WHISKEY RICKEY

1 ½ oz bourbon
½ oz lime juice
5 oz club soda
Orange slice

Combine bourbon and lime juice over ice in a highball glass. Add soda and stir. Garnish with orange slice.

*Stone Rickey*

*Whiskey Rickey*

## APPLE GINGER SANGAREE

1 ½ oz apple brandy

½ oz ginger wine

½ oz water

¼ oz simple syrup

Club soda

Lemon twist

Ground cinnamon

Ground nutmeg

In a highball glass, dissolve the syrup in the water and brandy. Fill with crushed ice and soda. Top with ginger wine and dust with cinnamon and nutmeg. Garnish with lemon twist.

## BOURBON SANGAREE

1 ½ oz bourbon

½ oz tawny port

½ oz water

¼ oz simple syrup

Club soda

Lemon twist

Ground cinnamon

Ground nutmeg

In a highball glass, dissolve the syrup in the water and bourbon. Fill with crushed ice and soda. Top with a float of port and dust with cinnamon and nutmeg. Garnish with lemon twist.

## BRANDY SANGAREE

1 ½ oz brandy

½ oz tawny port

½ oz water

¼ oz simple syrup

Club soda

Lemon twist

Ground cinnamon

Ground nutmeg

In a highball glass, dissolve the syrup in the water and brandy. Fill with crushed ice and soda. Top with a float of port and dust with cinnamon and nutmeg. Garnish with lemon twist.

## CREAM SHERRY SANGAREE

1 ½ oz cream sherry

½ oz Bénédictine

½ oz water

¼ oz simple syrup

Club soda

Ground cinnamon

Ground nutmeg

In a highball glass, dissolve the syrup in the water and sherry. Fill with crushed ice and soda. Top with a float of Bénédictine and dust with cinnamon and nutmeg.

## GIN SANGAREE

1 ½ oz gin

½ oz tawny port

½ oz water

¼ oz simple syrup

Club soda

Lemon twist

Ground cinnamon

Ground nutmeg

In a highball glass, dissolve the syrup in the water and gin. Fill with crushed ice and soda. Top with a float of port and dust with cinnamon and nutmeg. Garnish with lemon twist.

## MAPLE SANGAREE

1 oz bourbon

1 oz Calvados

½ oz water

1 oz maple simple syrup (2:1 maple syrup to water)

Club soda

Ground nutmeg

In a Collins or highball glass, dissolve syrup in the water, Calvados, and bourbon. Fill with crushed ice and soda. Dust with nutmeg.

## PEACH SANGAREE

1 ½ oz peach brandy

½ oz tawny port

½ oz water

¼ oz simple syrup

Club soda

Ground cinnamon

Ground nutmeg

In a highball glass, dissolve the syrup in the water and brandy. Fill with ice and soda. Top with a float of port and dust with cinnamon and nutmeg.

## PORT SANGAREE

2 oz tawny port

½ oz brandy

½ oz water

¼ oz simple syrup

Club soda

Ground cinnamon

Ground nutmeg

In a highball glass, dissolve the syrup in the water and port. Fill with crushed ice and soda. Top with a float of brandy and dust with cinnamon and nutmeg.

*Anise and cinnamon*

Port Sangaree

Port Sangaree

### SCOTCH SANGAREE

1 ½ oz Scotch whisky

½ oz tawny port

½ oz water

¼ oz simple syrup

Club soda

Lemon twist

Ground cinnamon

Ground nutmeg

In a highball glass, dissolve the syrup in the water and whisky. Fill with crushed ice and soda. Top with a float of port and dust with cinnamon and nutmeg. Garnish with lemon twist.

### STOUT SANGAREE

1 oz ruby port

12 oz stout

½ oz water

¼ oz simple syrup

Ground cinnamon

Ground nutmeg

In a beer mug, dissolve the syrup in the water. Fill with stout, creating a modest head. Top with a float of port and dust with cinnamon and nutmeg.

### WHISKEY SANGAREE

1 ½ oz whiskey of choice

½ oz tawny port

½ oz water

¼ oz simple syrup

Club soda

Lemon twist

Ground cinnamon

Ground nutmeg

In a highball glass, dissolve the syrup in the water and whiskey. Fill with crushed ice and soda. Top with a float of port and dust with cinnamon and nutmeg. Garnish with lemon twist.

*Stout Sangaree*

*Whiskey Sangaree*

## BOMBAY SLING

1 ½ oz brandy
½ oz cherry brandy
1 oz lemon juice
½ oz grenadine syrup
4 oz orange juice
Lemon peel
Maraschino cherry

Combine all ingredients and shake with ice. Strain into an ice-filled Collins or highball glass. Top with club soda if desired and garnish with lemon peel and cherry.

## CHAMBORD SLING

1 ½ oz gin
½ oz Chambord
1 oz lemon juice
¼ oz water
½ oz simple syrup
Lemon peel

Combine the gin, Chambord, water, lemon juice, and syrup and shake with ice. Strain into an ice-filled highball glass. Garnish with lemon peel.

## FLORIDA SLING

1 ½ oz gin
½ oz cherry brandy
1 ½ oz pineapple juice
¾ oz lemon juice
½ oz simple syrup
Dash of grenadine syrup
Lemon peel
Maraschino cherry

Combine gin, brandy, juices, and syrups and shake with ice. Strain into an ice-filled Collins or highball glass. Top with club soda if desired and garnish with lemon peel and cherry.

## BOURBON SLING

2 oz bourbon
1 oz lemon juice
¼ oz water
½ oz simple syrup
Lemon peel

Combine the bourbon, water, lemon juice, and syrup and shake with ice. Strain into an ice-filled highball glass. Garnish with lemon peel.

## CHERRY SLING

2 oz cherry brandy
1 oz lemon juice
¼ oz water
½ oz simple syrup
Lemon peel

Combine the brandy, water, lemon juice, and syrup and shake with ice. Strain into an ice-filled highball glass. Garnish with lemon peel.

## GIN SLING

2 oz gin
1 oz lemon juice
¼ oz water
½ oz simple syrup
Lemon peel

Combine the gin, water, lemon juice, and syrup and shake with ice. Strain into an ice-filled Collins or highball glass. Garnish with lemon peel.

## BRANDY SLING

2 oz brandy
1 oz lemon juice
¼ oz water
½ oz simple syrup
Lemon peel

Combine the brandy, water, lemon juice, and syrup and shake with ice. Strain into an ice-filled highball glass. Garnish with lemon peel.

## DARKWOOD SLING

2 oz cherry liqueur
1 oz orange juice
1 oz lemon juice
¼ oz water
½ oz simple syrup
Lemon peel

Combine the cherry liqueur, water, juices, and syrup and shake with ice. Strain into an ice-filled highball glass. Top with club soda if desired and garnish with lemon peel.

## HIGHLAND SLING

2 oz Highland Scotch whisky
1 oz lemon juice
¼ oz water
½ oz simple syrup
Lemon peel

Combine the whisky, water, lemon juice, and syrup and shake with ice. Strain into an ice-filled highball glass. Garnish with lemon peel.

*Gin Sling*

## IRON BAR SLING

1 oz gin

1 oz cherry brandy

¼ oz peach liqueur

2 oz orange juice

1 oz lime juice

1 oz pineapple juice

¼ oz grenadine syrup

Lemon peel

Combine the gin, brandy, peach liqueur, juices, and syrup and shake with ice. Strain into an ice-filled Collins or highball glass. Top with club soda if desired and garnish with lemon peel.

## MINERSTOWN SLING

1 oz dark rum

1 oz coffee liqueur

1 oz orange juice

½ oz simple syrup

Orange peel

Combine the rum, coffee liqueur, orange juice, and syrup and shake with ice. Strain into an ice-filled Collins or highball glass. Top with club soda if desired and garnish with orange peel.

## PAPAYA SLING

2 oz gin

1 oz lime juice

½ oz papaya juice

½ oz simple syrup

Dash of Angostura bitters

Pineapple wedge

Combine the gin, juices, and syrup and shake with ice. Strain into an ice-filled Collins or highball glass. Top with club soda if desired and garnish with pineapple wedge.

## POONA GIN SLING

2 oz gin

1 oz lemon juice

¼ oz water

½ oz simple syrup

Pinch of salt

Lemon peel

Combine the gin, water, lemon juice, syrup, and salt and shake with ice. Strain into an ice-filled Collins or highball glass. Garnish with lemon peel.

## RUM SLING

2 oz white rum

1 oz lemon juice

¼ oz water

½ oz simple syrup

Lemon peel

Combine the rum, water, lemon juice, and syrup and shake with ice. Strain into an ice-filled Collins or highball glass. Garnish with lemon peel.

## RYE SLING

2 oz rye whiskey

¼ oz cherry liqueur

1 oz lemon juice

¼ oz water

½ oz simple syrup

Lemon peel

Combine the whiskey, cherry liqueur, water, lemon juice, and syrup and shake with ice. Strain into an ice-filled Collins or highball glass. Garnish with lemon peel.

## SINGAPORE SLING

1 ½ oz gin

½ oz Cherry Heering

¼ oz Cointreau

¼ oz Bénédictine

½ oz lime juice

2 oz pineapple juice

2 dashes of grenadine syrup

Dash of Angostura bitters

Orange slice

Maraschino cherry

Combine gin, liqueurs, juices, syrup, and bitters and shake with ice. Strain into a highball glass. Top with club soda if desired and garnish with orange slice and cherry.

## SINGAPORE SLING CHINA GIRL

2 oz gin

1 oz cherry brandy

1 oz lemon juice

1 oz grenadine syrup

Dash of Angostura bitters

Orange slice

Maraschino cherry

Combine gin, brandy, juice, syrup, and bitters and shake with ice. Strain into a highball glass. Top with club soda if desired and garnish with orange slice and cherry.

*Singapore Sling*

*Texas Sling*

## SYDNEY SLING

1 ½ oz white rum
1 oz cherry brandy
½ oz triple sec
¼ oz Yellow Chartreuse
¾ oz lime juice
2 oz pineapple juice
1 ½ oz orange juice
Dash of Angostura bitters
Orange slice
Maraschino cherry

Shake rum, brandy, triple sec, Chartreuse, juices, and bitters with ice. Strain into a highball glass. Top with club soda if desired and garnish with orange slice and cherry.

## TEXAS SLING

2 oz bourbon
½ oz white rum
1 oz lemon juice
¼ oz water
½ oz simple syrup
Lemon peel

Combine the bourbon, rum, water, lemon juice, and syrup and shake with ice. Strain into an ice-filled Collins or highball glass. Garnish with lemon peel.

## VODKA SLING

2 oz vodka
1 oz lemon juice
¼ oz water
½ oz simple syrup
Lemon peel

Combine the vodka, water, lemon juice, and syrup and shake with ice. Strain into an ice-filled Collins or highball glass. Garnish with lemon peel.

## WESTERN SLING

2 oz gin
½ oz cherry brandy
1 oz lemon juice
½ oz simple syrup
¼ oz grenadine syrup
3 oz pineapple juice
Lemon peel

Combine the gin, brandy, juices, and syrups and shake with ice. Strain into an ice-filled Collins or highball glass. Top with club soda if desired and garnish with lemon peel.

## WHISKEY SLING

2 oz whiskey of choice
1 oz lemon juice
¼ oz water
½ oz simple syrup
Lemon peel

Combine the whiskey, water, lemon juice, and syrup and shake with ice. Strain into an ice-filled Collins or highball glass. Garnish with lemon peel.

*Whiskey Sling*

## APPLE SWIZZLE

1 ½ oz apple brandy

½ oz dark rum

3 oz sparkling apple juice

1 ½ oz lime juice

½ oz simple syrup

In the bottom of a Collins glass, dissolve the syrup into the lime juice. Fill glass with crushed ice and add brandy and rum. Top with apple juice and stir. Serve with a swizzle stick.

## GIN SWIZZLE

2 oz gin

1 ½ oz lime juice

1 oz simple syrup

2 dashes of Angostura bitters

3 oz club soda

In the bottom of a Collins glass, dissolve the syrup in the lime juice and soda. Fill the glass with crushed ice, add gin and bitters, and stir. Serve with a swizzle stick.

## RUM SWIZZLE

2 oz Barbados rum

1 ½ oz lime juice

1 oz simple syrup

2 dashes of Angostura bitters

3 oz club soda

In the bottom of a Collins glass, dissolve the syrup in the lime juice and soda. Fill the glass with crushed ice, add rum and bitters, and stir. Serve with a swizzle stick.

## BOURBON SWIZZLE

2 oz bourbon

1 ½ oz lime juice

1 oz simple syrup

2 dashes of Angostura bitters

3 oz club soda

In the bottom of a Collins glass, dissolve the syrup in the lime juice and soda. Fill the glass with crushed ice, add bourbon and bitters, and stir. Serve with a swizzle stick.

## MAI TAI SWIZZLE

1 ½ oz dark rum

1 oz white rum

½ oz triple sec

1 oz grapefruit juice

1 ½ oz lime juice

¼ oz almond syrup

Dash of Pernod

2 dashes of Angostura bitters

In the bottom of a Collins glass, stir together the almond syrup, lime juice, and grapefruit juice. Fill the glass with crushed ice, add rum, liqueurs, and bitters, and stir well. Serve with a swizzle stick.

## TARTAN SWIZZLE

2 oz Scotch whisky

1 ½ oz lime juice

1 oz simple syrup

2 dashes of Angostura bitters

3 oz club soda

In the bottom of a Collins glass, dissolve the syrup in the lime juice and soda. Fill the glass with crushed ice, add whisky and bitters, and stir. Serve with a swizzle stick.

## BRANDY SWIZZLE

2 oz brandy

1 ½ oz lime juice

1 oz simple syrup

2 dashes of Angostura bitters

3 oz club soda

In the bottom of a Collins glass, dissolve the syrup in the lime juice and soda. Fill the glass with crushed ice, add brandy and bitters, and stir. Serve with a swizzle stick.

## QUEEN'S PARK SWIZZLE

2 oz dark rum

1 ½ oz lime juice

1 oz simple syrup

2 dashes of Angostura bitters

3 oz club soda

3 mint leaves

In the bottom of a Collins glass, dissolve the syrup in the lime juice and soda. Drop in the mint leaves, fill the glass with crushed ice, add rum and bitters, and stir. Serve with a swizzle stick.

*Mai Tai Swizzle*

Alabazam

Bahama Mama

Bloody Mary

## ALABAZAM

2 oz brandy

½ oz orange curaçao

¾ oz lemon juice

½ oz simple syrup

2 dashes of Angostura
bitters

Club soda

Combine brandy, curaçao, lemon juice, syrup, and bitters and shake with ice. Strain into a highball glass over ice, top with soda, and stir.

## AMERICANO HIGHBALL

1 ½ oz sweet vermouth

1 ½ oz Campari

Club soda

Orange slice

Combine vermouth and Campari in an ice-filled highball glass, top with soda, and stir. Garnish with orange slice.

## AÑEJO HIGHBALL

1 ½ oz Añejo rum

½ oz orange curaçao

2 oz ginger beer

¼ oz lime juice

2 dashes of Angostura
bitters

Lime wheel

Orange slice

Combine rum, curaçao, lime juice, and bitters in a chilled highball glass. Top with ginger beer and garnish with lime wheel and orange slice.

## BAHAMA MAMA

½ oz dark rum

½ oz coconut liqueur

¼ oz overproof rum

¼ oz coffee liqueur

½ oz lemon juice

4 oz pineapple juice

Maraschino cherry

Combine rums, liqueurs, and juices and shake with ice. Strain into a highball glass over ice. Garnish with cherry.

## BAY BREEZE

3 oz vodka

1 oz cranberry juice

1 oz pineapple juice

Pineapple wedge

Combine vodka and juices and shake with ice. Strain into an ice-filled highball glass. Garnish with pineapple wedge.

## BLOODY BULL

1 ½ oz vodka

3 oz beef broth

2 oz tomato juice

4 dashes of Tabasco

Dash of orange juice

Dash of black pepper

Orange peel

Combine vodka, broth, juices, Tabasco, and pepper and shake with ice. Strain into a goblet or pint glass over ice. Garnish with orange peel.

## BLOODY CAESAR

1 ½ oz vodka

2 dashes of Worcestershire
sauce

4 dashes of Tabasco sauce

3 oz tomato juice

2 oz clam juice

¼ oz lemon juice

Lemon slice

Combine vodka, sauces, and juices in a mixing glass with ice and roll to mix. Strain into a large goblet or pint glass nearly filled with ice. Garnish with lemon slice.

## BLOODY MARIA

1 ½ oz tequila

4 oz Sangrita

¼ oz lemon juice

Lime slice

Combine tequila, Sangrita, and lemon juice in a mixing glass with ice and roll to mix. Strain into a large goblet or pint glass nearly filled with ice. Garnish with lime slice.

## BLOODY MARY

1 ½ oz vodka

2 dashes of Worcestershire
sauce

4 dashes of Tabasco sauce

4 oz tomato juice

¼ oz lemon juice

Pinch of salt and pepper

Lemon slice

Combine vodka, juices, sauces, and salt and pepper in a mixing glass with ice and roll to mix. Strain into a large goblet or pint glass nearly filled with ice. Garnish with lemon slice.

*Blue Lagoon*

## BLUE HAWAIIAN

1 oz light rum
1 oz blue curaçao
2 oz pineapple juice
1 oz cream of coconut
Pineapple wedge
Maraschino cherry

Combine rum, curaçao, juice, and cream of coconut with crushed ice and blend in a blender on high speed. Pour into a chilled highball or Collins glass. Garnish with pineapple wedge and cherry.

## BRAMBLE

1 ½ oz gin
¾ oz lime juice
¾ oz simple syrup
¾ oz crème de mure
Lime slice
Raspberries

Combine gin, lime juice, and syrup and shake with ice. Strain into a highball glass filled with crushed ice. Dribble the crème de mure so that it seeps down into the drink. Garnish with lime slice and raspberries.

## CHERRY HOOKER

1 oz cherry brandy
7 oz orange juice
¼ oz grenadine syrup
Orange slice
Maraschino cherry

Pour brandy, then orange juice, then grenadine into a Collins glass filled with ice. Garnish with orange slice and cherry.

## BLUE LAGOON

¾ oz white rum
¾ oz dark rum
½ oz blue curaçao
3 oz orange juice
3 oz pineapple juice
Dash of Angostura bitters
Pineapple wedge
Maraschino cherry

Shake rum, curaçao, juices, and bitters with ice. Strain into an ice-filled goblet or pint glass. Garnish with pineapple wedge and cherry.

## CAMPARI AND SODA

6 oz Campari
6 oz club soda

Pour Campari into a highball glass filled with ice. Top with club soda and stir.

## COGNAC AND SODA

2 oz Cognac
5 oz club soda
Lemon wedge

Pour Cognac into a highball glass over ice. Top with soda, stir, and garnish with lemon wedge.

## BOCCE BALL

1 ½ oz amaretto
5 oz orange juice
Orange slice

In a highball glass half-filled with ice, combine amaretto and orange juice. Garnish with orange slice.

## CAPE COD

1 ½ oz vodka
Cranberry juice
Lime wedge

Pour the vodka in a highball glass over ice. Top with cranberry juice, stir, and garnish with lime wedge.

## COLORADO BULLDOG

1 ½ oz Kahlúa
3 oz cold milk
3 oz cola

In a highball glass, build the Kahlúa and milk. Gently stir in the cola to fill, not letting the drink get too foamy.

## CRAWDADDY

1 ½ oz vodka

5 oz lemonade

Splash club soda

Lemon slice

Pour vodka over ice in a highball glass, top with lemonade, and stir. Garnish with lemon slice.

## DARK AND STORMY

2 oz dark rum

5 oz ginger beer

Lime wedge

Pour the rum over ice in a highball glass and fill with ginger beer. Squeeze in lime wedge.

## ELECTRIC ICED TEA

½ oz bourbon

½ oz gin

½ oz vodka

½ oz triple sec

4 oz cola

2 lemon wedges

Combine ingredients over ice in a highball glass, squeezing in the lemons. Stir.

## CREAMSICLE

1 ½ oz vanilla liqueur

3 oz orange juice

1 ½ oz milk

Combine all ingredients in a Collins glass, stir, and serve.

## DESERT HEALER

1 ½ oz gin

½ oz Cherry Heering

1 ½ oz orange juice

4 oz ginger ale

Orange peel

Cherry

Combine gin, Cherry Heering, and juice over ice in a highball glass. Fill with ginger ale and garnish with orange peel and cherry.

## FLORADORA

1 ½ oz gin

½ oz lime juice

¾ oz Framboise liqueur or raspberry syrup

Ginger ale

Lime wedge

Edible viola flower

Build the gin, lime juice, and Framboise in an ice-filled highball glass and top with ginger ale. Garnish with the lime wedge and viola flower.

## CUBA LIBRE

2 oz rum

¾ oz lime juice

Cola

Lime peel

Combine rum and lime juice in a Collins or highball glass. Top with ice and fill glass with cola. Garnish with lime peel.

## DESHLER COCKTAIL

1 ½ oz Red Dubonnet

1 ½ oz rye

¼ oz Cointreau

Dash of Angostura bitters

Orange peel

Shake the Dubonnet, rye, Cointreau, and bitters with ice and strain into a Collins glass. Add club soda if desired. Garnish with orange peel. Can also be served without soda as an "up" cocktail.

## FREDDIE FUDPUCKER

1 ½ oz tequila

5 oz orange juice

Galliano liqueur

Combine tequila and orange juice over ice in a highball glass. Top with a float of Galliano.

Cuba Libre

Dark and Stormy

## FRENCH 75

1 oz brandy
¾ oz simple syrup
½ oz lemon juice
Champagne

Combine brandy, syrup, and lemon juice and shake with ice. Strain into a goblet over ice. Top with champagne.

## FUZZY NAVEL

2 oz peach schnapps
5 oz orange juice
Seasonal fruit for garnish

Combine schnapps and juice over ice in a highball glass and garnish with fresh fruit.

## GREYHOUND

1 ½ oz vodka
4 oz grapefruit juice

Combine vodka and juice over ice in a highball glass.

## FRENCH 76

1 oz vodka
¾ oz simple syrup
½ oz lemon juice
Champagne

Combine vodka, syrup, and lemon juice and shake with ice. Strain into a goblet over ice. Top with champagne.

## GIN AND TONIC

2 oz gin
Tonic water
Lime wedge

Pour gin over ice in a highball glass and top with tonic water. Squeeze in lime wedge.

## HAIRY NAVEL

¾ oz vodka
¾ oz peach schnapps
5 oz orange juice
Seasonal fruit for garnish

Combine vodka, schnapps, and juice over ice in a highball glass and garnish with fresh fruit.

## FRENCH 95

1 oz bourbon
¾ oz simple syrup
½ oz lemon juice
1 oz orange juice
Champagne

Combine brandy, syrup, and juices and shake with ice. Strain into a goblet over ice. Top with champagne.

## GIN BUCK

1 ½ oz gin
1 oz lemon juice
Ginger ale
Lemon slice

Combine gin and lemon juice with ice in a highball glass and top with ginger ale. Garnish with lemon slice.

## HARVEY WALLBANGER

1 ½ oz vodka
4 oz orange juice
Galliano

Combine vodka and orange juice over ice in a highball glass. Top with a float of Galliano.

*Gin and Tonic*

*Harvey Wallbanger*

## HIGHBALL

2 oz liquor of choice

Soda, tonic water, or plain water

To be made quickly. Pour 2 oz liquor over ice in a highball glass and top with one mixer: any kind of soda, tonic water, or plain water. Garnish simply if desired.

## HOLLYWOOD

1 ½ oz vodka

1 ½ oz Chambord

1 oz triple sec

Splash lime juice

Club soda

Lime slice

Combine vodka, Chambord, and triple sec and shake with ice. Strain into a highball glass and top with soda. Garnish with lime slice. Can also be made as a short drink or "up" drink without soda.

## HORNY BULL

1 oz tequila

1 oz rum

1 oz simple syrup

Club soda

Lime slice

Combine tequila, rum, and syrup and shake with ice. Strain into a highball glass over ice and top with soda. Garnish with lime slice.

## HURRICANE

1 oz dark rum

1 oz light rum

½ oz Galliano

¾ oz lime juice

2 oz passion fruit syrup

2 oz orange juice

2 oz pineapple juice

1 oz simple syrup

Dash of Angostura bitters

Fresh tropical fruit for garnish

Combine rums, Galliano, juices, and syrups and shake with ice. Strain into an ice-filled hurricane glass and garnish with fresh fruit.

## LONG ISLAND ICED TEA

½ oz vodka

½ oz gin

½ oz rum

½ oz tequila

½ oz triple sec

¾ oz lemon juice

½ oz simple syrup

4 oz cola

Lemon wedge

Combine all liquids except cola and shake with ice. Strain into an ice-filled Collins glass, top with cola, and stir. Garnish with lemon wedge.

## LYNCHBURG LEMONADE

2 oz bourbon

1 oz Cointreau

1 oz lemon juice

Lemon-lime soda

Orange slice

Lemon wedge

Combine bourbon, Cointreau, and lemon juice and shake with ice. Strain into an ice-filled highball glass and top with soda. Garnish with orange slice and lemon wedge.

## MACHO GAZPACHO

1 ½ oz vodka

5 oz pureed gazpacho

Lemon wedge

Combine vodka and gazpacho and roll to mix. Pour into a goblet or pint glass over ice and garnish with lemon wedge.

## MADRAS

1 ½ oz vodka

4 oz orange juice

1 ½ oz cranberry juice cocktail drink

Orange slice

Build vodka and orange juice over ice in a highball glass. Float cranberry juice on top and garnish with orange slice.

## MALIBU BAY BREEZE

1 ½ oz Malibu rum

4 oz pineapple juice

1 ½ oz cranberry juice

Lime wedge

Ground nutmeg

Build the rum and juices in a highball glass over ice, garnish with lime wedge, and dust with nutmeg.

Hurricane

Lynchburg Lemonade

Long Island Iced Tea

## MELON BALL

¾ oz Midori melon liqueur

¾ oz vodka

5 oz orange juice

Orange slice

Melon slice

Combine Midori, vodka, and orange juice and shake with ice. Strain into an ice-filled highball glass and garnish with orange slice and, if possible, melon slice.

## MOSCOW MULE

1 ½ oz vodka

5 oz ginger beer

Lime wedge

Combine vodka and ginger beer over ice in a highball glass. Garnish with lime wedge.

## PIÑA COLADA

1 ½ oz light rum

1 oz dark rum

2 oz Coco Lopez

1 oz heavy cream

4 oz pineapple juice

Dash of Angostura bitters

1 cup crushed ice

Pineapple wedge

Maraschino cherry

Combine rums, Coco Lopez, cream, pineapple juice, bitters, and ice in a blender and blend for about 15 seconds. Pour into a specialty glass and garnish with the pineapple and cherry.

## MIAMI ICED TEA

½ oz vodka

½ oz gin

½ oz rum

½ oz peach schnapps

1 oz cranberry juice

Lemon-lime soda

Lemon wedge

Combine all ingredients except the soda and lemon and shake with ice. Strain into an ice-filled Collins glass, top with soda, stir, and garnish with lemon wedge.

## ORANGE JIMMY

1 ½ oz gold rum

¾ oz triple sec

½ oz Kahlúa

½ oz Madeira

4 oz orange juice

Orange slice

Combine rum, triple sec, Kahlúa, Madeira, and orange juice and shake with ice. Strain into a highball glass over ice and garnish with orange slice. Can also be served without orange juice as an "up" drink.

## PRESBYTERIAN

1 ½ oz bourbon

2 ½ oz club soda

2 ½ oz lemon-lime soda

Lemon peel

Combine the bourbon and sodas over ice in a highball glass. Garnish with lemon peel.

## MOJITO

1 ½ oz light rum

1 oz simple syrup

¾ oz lime juice

2 sprigs fresh mint

Club soda

Muddle one mint sprig with the syrup and lime juice in the bottom of a mixing glass. Add the rum and bitters and shake with ice. Strain into an ice-filled highball glass, top with soda, and garnish with mint sprig.

## PIMM'S CUP

1 ½ oz Pimm's No. 1

3 oz lemonade

Club soda

Apple slice

Cucumber spear

Combine Pimm's and lemonade in a highball glass over ice, fill with soda, and stir. Garnish with apple slice and cucumber spear.

## RED SNAPPER

2 oz gin

4 oz tomato juice

½ oz lemon juice

Pinch of salt and pepper

3 dashes Worcestershire sauce

2 drops Tabasco sauce

Celery stalk

Lemon wedge

Combine gin, juices, and spicy ingredients over ice in a highball glass and stir. Garnish with celery and lemon wedge.

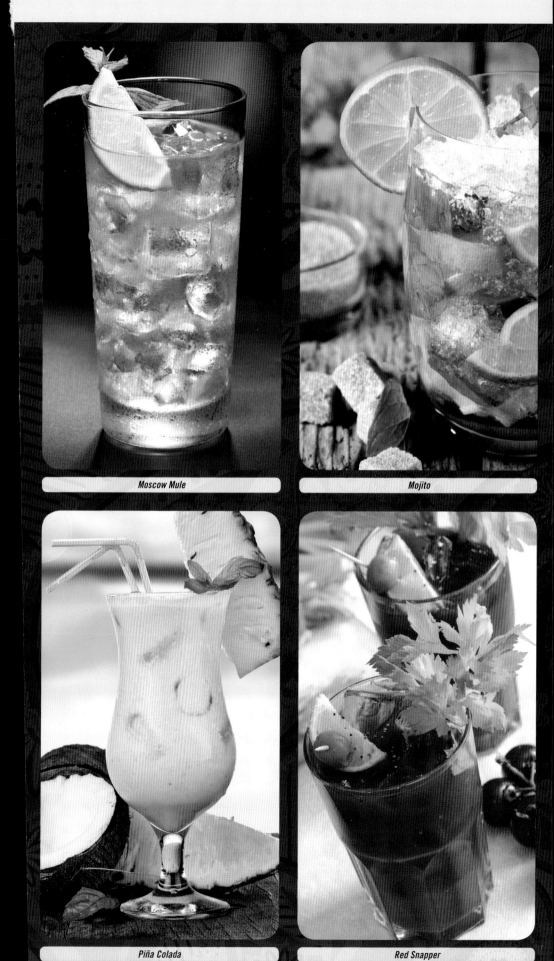

Moscow Mule

Mojito

Piña Colada

Red Snapper

Screwdriver

Rum Runner

Sex On The Beach

## RICARD TOMATE

2 oz Ricard

¼ oz grenadine syrup

4 oz water

Pour the Ricard and the grenadine into an empty highball glass and stir. Add water and then a few cubes of ice.

## SANGRITA

12 oz tomato juice

8 oz orange juice

2 ½ oz lime juice

1 ½ oz simple syrup

A few drops of Tabasco sauce

3 dashes white pepper

4 dashes salt

Combine all the ingredients and shake gently with ice so as not to make the drink too foamy. Strain over ice into an ice-filled Collins glass. Add 1 ½ oz vodka or tequila if desired, or use as a chaser after a tequila shot.

## SEA BREEZE

1 ½ oz vodka

4 oz grapefruit juice

1 ½ oz cranberry juice

Lime wedge

Pour the vodka into an ice-filled highball glass. Add the grapefruit juice and top with the cranberry juice. Garnish with lime wedge.

## RUM RUNNER

1 oz light rum

1 oz gold rum

1 oz pineapple juice

1 oz lime juice

1 oz simple syrup

Dash of Angostura bitters

Lime wedge

In the bottom of a mixing glass, bruise the lime wedge and then add the rums, juices, syrup, and bitters and shake well with ice. Serve over ice in a Collins glass, garnished with tropical fruits.

## SCOTCH AND SODA

2 oz Scotch whisky

Club soda

Lemon peel

Pour the Scotch into an ice-filled highball glass, top with soda, and stir. Garnish with lemon peel.

## SEVEN AND SEVEN

2 oz Seagram's 7 whiskey

5 oz 7-Up soda

Lemon peel

Combine whiskey and 7-Up over ice in a highball glass and stir. Garnish with orange slice.

## SALTY DOG

1 ½ oz vodka

Coarse salt, for glass rimming

Lime wedge, for glass rimming

Grapefruit juice

Rim a highball glass by rubbing the lime piece around the outside rim and then dusting the rim with coarse salt. Fill the glass with ice, add vodka, and fill with grapefruit juice.

## SCREWDRIVER

1 ½ oz vodka

8 oz orange juice

Orange slice

Combine vodka and orange juice over ice in a highball glass and stir. Garnish with orange slice.

## SEX ON THE BEACH

1 ½ oz vodka

½ oz peach schnapps

¼ oz Chambord

2 oz cranberry juice

2 oz pineapple juice

Combine all ingredients and shake with ice. Strain into a highball glass over ice.

## SLOE COMFORTABLE SCREW

1 ½ oz vodka

1 oz sloe gin

½ oz Southern Comfort

4 oz orange juice

Orange slice

Combine vodka, gin, Southern Comfort, and orange juice over ice in a highball glass and stir. Garnish with orange slice.

## SOUTHSIDE

2 oz gin

¾ oz lime juice

1 oz simple syrup

2 sprigs fresh mint

2 lime wedges

4 oz club soda

In the bottom of a mixing glass, muddle one of the mint sprigs with the limes, lime juice, and syrup. Add the gin and shake well. Pour into a goblet over crushed ice and stir well. Top with soda and garnish with mint.

## TEXAS TEA

2 oz tequila

2 oz rum

2 oz vodka

2 oz gin

2 oz bourbon

2 oz triple sec

1 oz lemon juice

¾ oz simple syrup

Cola

Combine all the ingredients but the cola in a pitcher filled with ice and stir. Then add the cola and stir well. Serve in an ice-filled Collins or highball glass.

## SMITH AND KEARNS

2 oz Kahlúa

3 oz light cream

Club soda

Combine Kahlúa and light cream over ice in a highball glass and top with soda.

## SUNFLOWER HIGHBALL

1 oz vodka

1 oz Licor 43

5 oz orange juice

Grated nutmeg

Combine vodka, Licor 43, and orange juice over ice in a highball glass. Dust with nutmeg.

## TIJUANA TAXI

2 oz gold tequila

1 oz Blue Curaçao

1 oz tropical fruit schnapps

Lemon-lime soda

Orange slice

Combine tequila, Blue Curaçao, and schnapps in an ice-filled highball glass and stir. Fill with soda and garnish with orange slice.

## SMITH AND WESSON

1 oz vodka

1 oz Kahlúa

1 oz light cream

Cola

Combine vodka, Kahlúa, and cream over ice in a highball glass and top with cola.

## TEQUILA SUNRISE

1 ½ oz white tequila

4 oz lemon juice

Simple syrup

Grenadine syrup

Using the syrup, sweeten the lemon juice to taste. Then pour tequila and then the lemon juice over ice in a highball glass. Top with a float of grenadine.

## TYPHOON

1 oz gin

½ oz anisette

1 oz lime juice

Champagne, chilled

Combine the gin, anisette, and lime juice and shake with ice. Strain into an ice-filled Collins glass and top with champagne.

Tequila Sunrise

Zombie

*Vodka Tonic*

## VODKA RED BULL

2 oz vodka

5 oz Red Bull energy drink

Combine the vodka and Red Bull in an ice-filled highball glass.

## VODKA TONIC

2 oz vodka

5 oz tonic water

Lime wedge

Combine vodka and tonic water in an ice-filled highball glass and stir. Garnish with the lime wedge.

## ZOMBIE

1 oz dark rum

1 oz light rum

1 oz orange curaçao

½ oz lime juice

1 oz lemon juice

1 ½ oz passion fruit purée

¼ oz grenadine syrup

Dash of Angostura bitters

Sprig of fresh mint

Combine the liquors, curaçao, juices, purée, syrup, and bitters in a mixing glass and shake with ice. Strain into a highball glass and garnish with mint and, if desired, seasonal fruit.

# SHORT
# DRINKS

AS YOU MIGHT IMAGINE, A SHORT DRINK IS SIMPLY A
DRINK SERVED IN A TUMBLER OR OLD-FASHIONED GLASS.
SINCE THEY CONTAIN A HIGHER CONCENTRATION OF
ALCOHOL THAN LONG DRINKS, THEY TEND TO BE BUILT
MORE FOR SLOW, DELIBERATE SIPPING—BUT THERE ARE
NO HARD AND FAST RULES HERE.

## BOURBON COBBLER

2 ½ oz bourbon

½ oz lemon juice

¼ oz grapefruit juice

¼ oz almond extract

Peach slice

Combine all ingredients but the peach slice in a mixing glass. Pour into ice-filled old-fashioned glass. Garnish with a slice of peach.

## CLARET COBBLER

3 oz claret or other dry red wine

2 oz club soda

¼ oz simple syrup

Lemon slice

Dissolve syrup in club soda in a red wine glass. Add claret, then top with ice and stir. Garnish with lemon slice.

## PORT COBBLER

3 oz ruby port

Club soda

¼ oz simple syrup

2 orange slices

2 lemon slices

Muddle one each of the fruit pieces with the simple syrup in the bottom of a mixing glass. Add the port, shake with ice, and strain into a double old-fashioned glass nearly filled with crushed ice. Top with club soda and garnish with remaining fruit.

## BRANDY COBBLER

2 oz brandy or Cognac

¼ oz raspberry syrup or liqueur

2 oz club soda

Orange slice

Lemon slice

Blend raspberry syrup or liqueur with club soda in a double old-fashioned glass. Fill glass with shaved ice, then brandy or Cognac, and stir. Garnish with the fruit wedges.

## GIN COBBLER

2 oz gin

2 oz club soda

¼ oz simple syrup

Lemon slice

Dissolve syrup in club soda in a red wine glass. Add gin, then top with ice and stir. Garnish with lemon slice.

## RUM COBBLER

2 oz light rum

2 oz club soda

¼ oz simple syrup

Orange slice

Lemon slice

Dissolve syrup in club soda in an old-fashioned glass. Fill glass with crushed ice. Add rum and stir. Garnish with fruit slices.

## CHERRY COBBLER

2 oz dry gin

1 ½ oz cherry brandy

⅛ oz crème de cassis

¾ oz simple syrup

¾ oz lemon juice

Lemon slice

Cherry

Combine gin, brandy, crème de cassis, syrup, and juice with ice in a mixing glass and shake. Strain into a double old-fashioned glass filled with ice. Garnish with lemon slice and cherry.

## JAPANESE COBBLER

3 oz sake

½ oz maraschino liqueur

Club soda

2 pineapple wedges

2 orange slices

2 lemon slices

Muddle one each of the fruit pieces with the maraschino liqueur in a mixing glass. Add the sake and shake with ice. Strain into a double old-fashioned glass filled with crushed ice. Top with club soda and garnish with remaining fruit.

## SCORPINO

2 oz vodka

2 oz cream

1 oz Cointreau or triple sec

1 scoop lemon Italian ice

Blend all the ingredients and serve in a double old-fashioned or other large glass.

*Claret Cobbler*

*Whiskey Cobbler*

### SCOTCH COBBLER

2 oz Scotch whisky

Curaçao or triple sec

Brandy

Orange slice

Combine whisky with a splash each of Curaçao and brandy in an old-fashioned glass. Fill glass with crushed ice and stir. Garnish with orange slice.

### SHERRY COBBLER

3 oz medium sherry

½ oz maraschino liqueur

½ oz lemon juice

2 oz orange juice

Orange slice

Lemon slice

Combine sherry, liqueur, and juices with ice and shake. Strain into a double old-fashioned or similar glass filled with crushed ice. Garnish with fruit slices.

### WHISKEY COBBLER

2 oz whiskey of choice

¾ oz Curaçao or triple sec

½ oz lemon juice

Orange slice

Lemon slice

Combine whiskey, Curaçao, and lemon juice with ice and shake. Strain into a double old-fashioned glass filled with crushed ice. Garnish with fruit slices.

*Lemon slices*

## APPLEJACK DAISY

2 oz Applejack brandy

1 oz lime juice

⅛ oz grenadine syrup

⅛ oz simple syrup

Lemon slice

Maraschino cherry

Combine brandy, lime juice, and syrups and shake with ice. Strain into an ice-filled old-fashioned glass. Garnish with lemon slice and cherry.

## CANADIAN DAISY

2 oz Canadian whisky

⅛ oz brandy

½ oz lemon juice

⅛ oz raspberry syrup

2 raspberries

Combine whisky, lemon juice, and raspberry syrup and shake with ice. Strain into an ice-filled old-fashioned glass. Float brandy on top and garnish with raspberries.

## DETROIT DAISY

2 oz dark rum

1 oz lime juice

⅛ oz simple syrup

⅛ oz grenadine syrup

Sprig of mint

Combine rum, lemon juice, and syrups and shake with ice. Strain into an ice-filled old-fashioned glass. Garnish with spring of mint.

## BOURBON DAISY

2 oz bourbon

1 oz lemon juice

⅛ oz grenadine syrup

⅛ oz simple syrup

Orange slice

Maraschino cherry

Combine bourbon, lemon juice, and syrups and shake with ice. Strain into an ice-filled old-fashioned glass. Garnish with orange slice and cherry.

## CHAMPAGNE DAISY

1 ½ oz Yellow Chartreuse

1 oz lemon juice

⅛ oz grenadine syrup

Brut champagne

Lemon slice

Maraschino cherry

Combine Chartreuse, lemon juice, and syrup and shake with ice. Strain into an ice-filled old-fashioned glass. Top with champagne, stir, and garnish with lemon slice and cherry.

## GIN DAISY

2 oz gin

1 oz lemon juice

⅛ oz grenadine syrup

⅛ oz simple syrup

Maraschino cherry

Orange slice

Combine gin, lemon juice, and syrups and shake with ice. Strain into an ice-filled old-fashioned glass. Garnish with orange slice and cherry.

## BRANDY DAISY

2 oz brandy

1 oz lemon juice

⅛ oz grenadine syrup

⅛ oz simple syrup

Orange slice

Maraschino cherry

Combine brandy, lemon juice, and syrups and shake with ice. Strain into an ice-filled old-fashioned glass. Garnish with orange slice and cherry.

## DAISY DUELLER

1 ½ oz Tennessee whiskey

1 ½ oz lemon juice

1 oz simple syrup

A few drops of Cointreau or triple sec

Club soda

Lemon slice

Combine whiskey, lemon juice, Cointreau, and syrup and shake with ice. Pour into a chilled old-fashioned glass. Add ice and top with club soda. Garnish with lemon slice.

## LEMON DAISY

2 oz lemon vodka

1 oz lemon juice

⅛ oz grenadine syrup

⅛ oz simple syrup

Club soda

Maraschino cherry

Lime slice

Combine vodka, lemon juice, and syrups and shake with ice. Strain into an ice-filled old-fashioned glass. Top with club soda, stir, and garnish with lime slice and cherry.

*Canadian Daisy*

## MAY DAISY

2 oz Cognac or Armagnac

1 oz lemon juice

¾ oz Green Chartreuse

¾ oz simple syrup

Sprig of mint

Combine Cognac, Chartreuse, lemon juice, and syrup and shake with ice. Strain into an ice-filled old-fashioned glass. Garnish with mint sprig.

## SAVOY DAISY

2 oz ruby port

¼ oz gold rum

1 oz dark rum

1 oz lemon juice

⅛ oz simple syrup

⅛ oz grenadine syrup

Orange peel

Combine port, rums, lemon juice, and syrups and shake with ice. Strain into a chilled old-fashioned glass. Garnish with orange peel.

## WHISKEY DAISY

1 ½ oz bourbon

½ oz Yellow Chartreuse

¾ oz simple syrup

2 lemon wedges

2 lime wedges

Maraschino cherry

In a mixing glass, muddle one each of the wedges with the syrup and Chartreuse. Add whiskey and shake with ice. Strain into an ice-filled old-fashioned glass. Garnish with remaining wedges and the cherry.

## PORTUGUESE DAISY

2 oz ruby port

1 oz brandy

1 oz lemon juice

⅛ oz grenadine syrup

⅛ oz simple syrup

Lemon slice

Combine port, brandy, lemon juice, and syrups and shake with ice. Strain into an ice-filled old-fashioned glass. Garnish with lemon slice.

## SCOTCH DAISY

2 oz Scotch whisky

1 oz lemon juice

⅛ oz grenadine syrup

⅛ oz simple syrup

Maraschino cherry

Orange slice

Combine whisky, lemon juice, and syrups and shake with ice. Strain into an ice-filled old-fashioned glass. Garnish with orange slice and cherry.

## WHOOPSIE DAISY

2 oz blueberry vodka

1 ½ oz triple sec

1 oz lemon juice

¼ oz simple syrup

⅛ oz grenadine syrup

Lime slice

Combine vodka, triple sec, lemon juice, and syrups and shake with ice. Strain into an ice-filled old-fashioned glass. Garnish with lime slice.

## RUM DAISY

2 oz dark rum

1 oz lemon juice

⅛ oz grenadine syrup

⅛ oz simple syrup

Maraschino cherry

Lemon slice

Combine rum, lemon juice, and syrups and shake with ice. Strain into an ice-filled old-fashioned glass. Garnish with lemon slice and cherry.

## VODKA DAISY

2 oz vodka

1 oz lemon juice

⅛ oz grenadine syrup

⅛ oz simple syrup

Maraschino cherry

Orange slice

Combine vodka, lemon juice, and syrups and shake with ice. Strain into an ice-filled old-fashioned glass. Garnish with orange slice and cherry.

Scotch Daisy

## BOURBON FLIP

1 ½ oz bourbon
1 tsp superfine sugar
1 small whole egg
Grated nutmeg

Combine all ingredients but nutmeg in a mixing glass and shake well with ice. Strain into a sour glass and dust with nutmeg.

## COFFEE FLIP

1 oz brandy
1 oz port
1 tsp superfine sugar
1 small whole egg
Grated nutmeg

Combine all ingredients but nutmeg in a mixing glass and shake well with ice. Strain into a sour glass and dust with nutmeg.

## PORTO FLIP

1 ½ oz bourbon
1 tsp superfine sugar
1 small whole egg
¼ oz Bénédictine
Grated nutmeg

Combine all ingredients but nutmeg in a mixing glass and shake well with ice. Strain into a sour glass and dust with nutmeg.

## BRANDY FLIP

1 ½ oz brandy
1 tsp superfine sugar
1 small whole egg
Grated nutmeg

Combine all ingredients but nutmeg in a mixing glass and shake well with ice. Strain into a sour glass and dust with nutmeg.

## COGNAC FLIP

1 ½ oz Cognac
1 tsp superfine sugar
1 small whole egg
Grated nutmeg

Combine all ingredients but nutmeg in a mixing glass and shake well with ice. Strain into a sour glass and dust with nutmeg.

## PORT WINE FLIP

2 oz port
1 tsp superfine sugar
1 small whole egg
Grated nutmeg

Combine all ingredients but nutmeg in a mixing glass and shake well with ice. Strain into a sour glass and dust with nutmeg.

## CHERRY FLIP

1 ½ oz cherry brandy
1 tsp superfine sugar
1 small whole egg
Grated nutmeg

Combine all ingredients but nutmeg in a mixing glass and shake well with ice. Strain into a sour glass and dust with nutmeg.

## CREAM SHERRY FLIP

2 ½ oz cream sherry
1 tsp superfine sugar
1 small whole egg
½ oz light cream
Grated nutmeg

Combine all ingredients but nutmeg in a mixing glass and shake well with ice. Strain into a sour glass and dust with nutmeg.

## SCOTCH FLIP

1 ½ oz Scotch whisky
1 tsp superfine sugar
1 small whole egg
Grated nutmeg

Combine all ingredients but nutmeg in a mixing glass and shake well with ice. Strain into a sour glass and dust with nutmeg.

Porto Flip

*Sherry Flip*

### SHERRY FLIP

1 ½ oz medium sherry

1 tsp superfine sugar

1 small whole egg

½ oz light cream

¼ oz light crème de cacao

Grated nutmeg

Combine all ingredients but nutmeg in a mixing glass and shake well with ice. Strain into a sour glass and dust with nutmeg.

### SLOE GIN FLIP

1 ½ oz sloe gin

1 tsp superfine sugar

1 small whole egg

Grated nutmeg

Combine all ingredients but nutmeg in a mixing glass and shake well with ice. Strain into a sour glass and dust with nutmeg.

### WHISKEY FLIP

1 ½ oz whiskey of choice

1 tsp superfine sugar

1 small whole egg

Grated nutmeg

Combine all ingredients but nutmeg in a mixing glass and shake well with ice. Strain into a sour glass and dust with nutmeg.

*Sloe Gin Flip*

## ABSINTHE CURAÇAO FRAPPE

1 oz absinthe
½ oz Blue Curaçao
½ oz lemon juice
1 oz orange juice
Slice orange

Stir together absinthe, curaçao, and juices and pour into a pousse café glass filled with crushed ice. Garnish with orange slice.

## BANANA RUM FRAPPE

2 oz light rum
1 oz banana liqueur
1 oz orange juice

Combine ingredients and pour into a pousse café glass filled with crushed ice.

## CAFÉ ROYAL FRAPPE

1 oz Cognac
3 oz chilled black coffee

Combine ingredients and pour into a pousse café glass filled with crushed ice.

## ALL WHITE FRAPPE

1 oz anisette
1 oz light crème de cacao
½ oz white crème de menthe
¼ oz lemon juice

Combine ingredients and pour into a pousse café glass filled with crushed ice.

## BANANA STRAWBERRY FRAPPE

1 ½ oz banana liqueur
1 oz strawberry yogurt
1 tsp lemon juice

Combine ingredients in a blender and blend until pureed. Pour over crushed ice in a pousse café glass.

## CAPTAIN'S FRAPPE

2 oz crème de cacao
1 cup chilled black coffee
½ oz simple syrup

Combine ingredients and pour into a pousse café glass filled with crushed ice.

## AMARETTO FRAPPE

2 oz amaretto
Crushed ice

Pour the amaretto into a pousse café glass filled with crushed ice.

## BRANDIED APRICOT FRAPPE

¾ oz brandy
¼ oz crème de noyeau
½ oz apricot brandy

Combine ingredients and pour into a pousse café glass filled with crushed ice.

## CHOCOLATE ORANGE FRAPPE

¾ oz crème de cacao
¾ oz orange juice
¼ oz Galliano

Combine ingredients and pour into a pousse café glass filled with crushed ice.

*Café Royal Frappe*

*Coffee Frappe*

## CHOCOLATE PEPPERMINT FRAPPE

1 ½ oz chocolate liqueur

½ oz white crème de menthe

1 shot espresso, chilled

Combine ingredients and pour into a pousse café glass filled with crushed ice.

## COGNAC MINT FRAPPE

1 oz Cognac

¾ oz white crème de menthe

Combine ingredients and pour into a pousse café glass filled with crushed ice.

## LEMON FRAPPE

1 oz gin

¾ oz limoncello

½ oz lemon juice

Simple syrup

Dissolve syrup into lemon juice until sweet to taste. Combine ingredients and pour into a pousse café glass filled with crushed ice.

## COCONUT FRAPPE

1 ½ oz Bailey's Irish Cream

¾ oz coconut rum

1 oz light cream or milk

Combine ingredients in a mixing glass, shake well, and pour into a pousse café glass filled with crushed ice.

## FRUIT FRAPPE

1 oz vodka

1 oz orange juice

½ oz mango nectar

½ oz crème de banane

Combine ingredients and pour into a pousse café glass filled with crushed ice.

## MANGO FRAPPE

1 oz light rum

1 oz mango nectar

½ oz lime juice

Combine ingredients and pour into a pousse café glass filled with crushed ice.

## COFFEE FRAPPE

1 ½ oz Kahlúa

1 tsp instant coffee

2 tsp superfine sugar

Combine ingredients and pour into a pousse café glass filled with crushed ice.

## FRUIT RUM FRAPPE

1 ½ oz white rum

½ oz crème de banane

¾ oz orange juice

½ oz mango nectar

½ oz lime juice

Combine ingredients and pour into a pousse café glass filled with crushed ice.

## MOCHA FRAPPE

¾ oz coffee liqueur

¼ oz white crème de menthe

¼ oz crème de cacao

¼ oz triple sec

Combine ingredients and pour into a pousse café glass filled with crushed ice.

## ABC POUSSE CAFÉ

½ oz amaretto

½ oz Bailey's Irish Cream

½ oz Cointreau

Layer liqueurs in the order listed from the bottom to the top of a cordial glass.

## MELON POUSSE CAFÉ

1 oz amaretto

1 oz crème de cacao

1 oz Midori melon liqueur

Layer liqueurs in the order listed from the bottom to the top of a cordial glass.

## POUSSE CAFÉ À LA FRANCAISE

½ oz Green Chartreuse

½ oz maraschino liqueur

½ oz cherry brandy

½ oz Kummel caraway liqueur

Layer liqueurs in the order listed from the bottom to the top of a cordial glass.

## AMERICAN FLAG POUSSE CAFÉ

1 oz grenadine syrup

1 oz orange liqueur

1 oz maraschino liqueur

Layer liqueurs in the order listed from the bottom to the top of a cordial glass.

## PARISIAN POUSSE CAFÉ

¾ oz cherry brandy

¾ oz orange curaçao

¾ oz Cognac

¾ oz Green Chartreuse

Layer liqueurs in the order listed from the bottom to the top of a cordial glass.

## POUSSE CAFÉ STANDISH

½ oz grenadine syrup

½ oz white crème de menthe

½ oz Galliano

½ oz Kummel caraway liqueur

½ oz brandy

¾ oz Cognac

Layer ingredients in the order listed from the bottom to the top of a cordial glass.

## KING ALFONSE

1 ½ oz dark crème de cacao

2 oz heavy cream

Layer the heavy cream over the crème de cacao in a cordial glass.

*King Alfonse*

114

*American Flag Pousse Café*

## POUSSE L'AMOUR

1 oz maraschino liqueur

1 egg yolk

1 oz Galliano

1 oz brandy

Layer ingredients in the order listed from the bottom to the top of a cordial glass.

## POUSSE MOZART

1 oz Mozart white chocolate liqueur

1 oz Mozart original chocolate liqueur

Layer the original chocolate liqueur over the white chocolate liqueur in a cordial glass.

## PRINCESS POUSSE CAFÉ

¾ oz apricot brandy

¼ oz heavy cream

Layer the cream above the brandy in a cordial glass.

*ABC Pousse Café*

*Princess Pousse Café*

## ABSOLUTELY CRANBERRY SMASH

2 oz vodka

4 oz cranberry juice

Club soda

½ oz simple syrup

4 sprigs mint

Combine all ingredients but the soda in a mixer and shake well with ice. Strain into an old-fashioned glass over ice and top with soda if desired. Garnish with mint and fruit if desired.

## BLUEBERRY SMASH

2 oz blueberry vodka

½ oz simple syrup

4 sprigs fresh mint

Club soda

Combine all ingredients but the soda in a mixer and shake well with ice. Strain into an old-fashioned glass over ice and top with soda if desired. Garnish with mint and fruit if desired.

## CHERRY SMASH

2 oz vodka

½ oz Cherry Heering

½ oz simple syrup

4 sprigs fresh mint

Club soda

Combine all ingredients but the soda in a mixer and shake well with ice. Strain into an old-fashioned glass over ice and top with soda if desired. Garnish with mint and fruit if desired.

## ARUBA SMASH

2 oz light rum

1 oz lemon juice

1 oz lime juice

4 sprigs fresh mint

Club soda

Combine all ingredients but the soda in a mixer and shake well with ice. Strain into an old-fashioned glass over ice and top with soda if desired. Garnish with mint and fruit if desired.

## BOURBON SMASH

2 oz bourbon

½ oz simple syrup

4 sprigs fresh mint

Club soda

Combine all ingredients but the soda in a mixer and shake well with ice. Strain into an old-fashioned glass over ice and top with soda if desired. Garnish with mint and fruit if desired.

## CHOCO BANANA SMASH

1 ½ oz chocolate liqueur

½ oz banana liqueur

¼ oz Galliano

½ oz simple syrup

4 sprigs fresh mint

Combine all ingredients in a mixer and shake well with ice. Strain into an old-fashioned glass over ice.

## BAHAMIAN GOOMBAY SMASH

¾ oz coconut rum

1 oz dark rum

¼ oz triple sec

¼ oz lemon juice

½ oz simple syrup

2 oz pineapple juice

Club soda

Several mint leaves

Combine all ingredients but the soda in a mixer and shake well with ice. Strain into an old-fashioned glass over ice and top with soda if desired. Garnish with fruit if desired.

## BRANDY SMASH

2 oz brandy

½ oz simple syrup

4 sprigs fresh mint

Club soda

Combine all ingredients but the soda in a mixer and shake well with ice. Strain into an old-fashioned glass over ice and top with soda if desired. Garnish with mint and fruit if desired.

## CHOCOLATE MINT SMASH

2 oz chocolate liqueur

½ oz simple syrup

4 sprigs fresh mint

Combine all ingredients in a mixer and shake well with ice. Strain into an old-fashioned glass over ice.

*Absolutely Cranberry Smash*

## CRANBERRY SMASH

2 oz gin

4 oz cranberry juice

½ oz simple syrup

4 sprigs fresh mint

Club soda

Combine all ingredients but the soda in a mixer and shake well with ice. Strain into an old-fashioned glass over ice and top with soda if desired. Garnish with mint.

## GOOMBAY SMASH

1 oz light rum

1 oz dark rum

½ oz coconut rum

1 oz pineapple juice

½ oz simple syrup

4 sprigs fresh mint

Club soda

Combine all ingredients but the soda in a mixer and shake well with ice. Strain into an old-fashioned glass over ice and top with soda if desired. Garnish with mint.

## GRAPEFRUIT PINEAPPLE SMASH

2 oz light rum

2 oz grapefruit juice

1 oz pineapple juice

½ oz simple syrup

4 sprigs fresh mint

Club soda

Combine all ingredients but the soda in a mixer and shake well with ice. Strain into an old-fashioned glass over ice and top with soda if desired. Garnish with mint.

## FRUITY SMASH

2 oz cherry brandy

1 oz pineapple juice

½ oz simple syrup

4 sprigs fresh mint

Club soda

Combine all ingredients but the soda in a mixer and shake well with ice. Strain into an old-fashioned glass over ice and top with soda if desired. Garnish with mint.

## GOOMBAY SMASH NASSAU

1 oz light rum

1 oz coconut rum

2 oz pineapple juice

1 oz orange juice

½ oz simple syrup

4 sprigs fresh mint

Club soda

Combine all ingredients but the soda in a mixer and shake well with ice. Strain into an old-fashioned glass over ice and top with soda if desired. Garnish with mint.

## ISLAND SMASH

2 oz light rum

½ oz banana liqueur

½ oz lime juice

1 oz orange juice

½ oz simple syrup

4 sprigs fresh mint

Club soda

Combine all ingredients but the soda in a mixer and shake well with ice. Strain into an old-fashioned glass over ice and top with soda if desired. Garnish with mint.

## GIN SMASH

2 oz gin

½ oz simple syrup

4 sprigs fresh mint

Club soda

Combine all ingredients but the soda in a mixer and shake well with ice. Strain into an old-fashioned glass over ice and top with soda if desired. Garnish with mint.

## GOOMBAY SMASH CHARLESTON

1 ½ oz light rum

1 oz banana liqueur

2 oz pineapple juice

2 oz orange juice

½ oz simple syrup

4 sprigs fresh mint

Club soda

Combine all ingredients but the soda in a mixer and shake well with ice. Strain into an old-fashioned glass over ice and top with soda if desired. Garnish with mint.

## ITALIAN SMASH

2 oz brandy

½ oz chocolate liqueur

1 shot espresso, chilled

4 sprigs fresh mint

Coffee beans

Combine all ingredients in a mixer and shake well with ice. Strain into an old-fashioned glass over ice. Garnish with coffee beans.

*Grapefruit Pineapple Smash*

## MALIBU SMASH

1 oz vodka

1 oz peach schnapps

1 oz coconut rum

2 oz orange juice

½ oz grenadine syrup

4 sprigs fresh mint

Combine all ingredients in a mixer and shake well with ice. Strain into an old-fashioned glass over ice. Garnish with mint if desired.

## ORANGE SMASH

1 oz light rum

1 oz triple sec

1 oz simple syrup

4 sprigs fresh mint

Club soda

Combine all ingredients but the soda in a mixer and shake well with ice. Strain into an old-fashioned glass over ice and top with soda if desired. Garnish with mint.

## RASPBERRY LIME SMASH

1 ½ oz vodka

¾ oz Chambord

1 oz simple syrup

4 sprigs fresh mint

Club soda

Combine all ingredients but the soda in a mixer and shake well with ice. Strain into an old-fashioned glass over ice and top with soda if desired. Garnish with mint.

## MANDARIN CHERRY SMASH

1 ½ oz orange vodka

¾ oz cherry brandy

4 sprigs fresh mint

½ oz simple syrup

Combine all ingredients in a mixer and shake well with ice. Strain into an old-fashioned glass over ice. Garnish with mint if desired.

## ORANGE VANILLA SMASH

1 oz light rum

1 oz triple sec

½ oz Galliano

1 oz simple syrup

4 sprigs fresh mint

Club soda

Combine all ingredients but the soda in a mixer and shake well with ice. Strain into an old-fashioned glass over ice and top with soda if desired. Garnish with mint.

## RASPBERRY ORANGE SMASH

1 oz vodka

½ oz Chambord

½ oz Grand Marnier

1 oz simple syrup

4 sprigs fresh mint

Combine all ingredients in a mixer and shake well with ice. Strain into an old-fashioned glass over ice. Garnish with mint if desired.

## OP SMASH

1 ½ oz OP vodka

¼ oz maraschino liqueur

¾ oz simple syrup

4 sprigs fresh mint

Club soda

Combine all ingredients but the soda in a mixer and shake well with ice. Strain into an old-fashioned glass over ice and top with soda if desired. Garnish with mint.

## POMEGRANATE SMASH

1 ½ oz vodka

¾ oz pomegranate liqueur

½ oz simple syrup

4 sprigs fresh mint

Club soda

Combine all ingredients but the soda in a mixer and shake well with ice. Strain into an old-fashioned glass over ice and top with soda if desired. Garnish with mint.

*Raspberry Lime Smash*

### TEA LEMON SMASH

1 ½ oz gin

¾ oz limoncello

3 oz strong iced tea

1 oz simple syrup

4 sprigs fresh mint

Combine all ingredients in a mixer and shake well with ice. Strain into an old-fashioned glass over ice. Garnish with mint if desired.

### WHISKEY PEACH SMASH

2 oz whiskey

¾ oz peach schnapps

1 oz simple syrup

4 sprigs fresh mint

Club soda

Lemon wedge

Combine all ingredients but the soda in a mixer and shake well with ice. Strain into an old-fashioned glass over ice and top with soda if desired. Garnish with mint and a lemon wedge.

### WHISKEY SMASH

2 ½ oz whiskey

1 oz simple syrup

4 sprigs fresh mint

Club soda

Lemon peel

Combine all ingredients but the soda in a mixer and shake well with ice. Strain into an old-fashioned glass over ice and top with soda if desired. Garnish with mint and lemon peel.

*Whiskey Peach Smash*

*Whiskey Smash*

# LITERARY COCKTAILS

Literature has its own compendium of cocktails, both on the page and in the hands of writers— typing or scribbling away with a favorite drink within reach, or schmoozing with fellow artists in the bars of Paris, London, or New York.

## FITZGERALD AND HEMINGWAY

No two writers are more intimately associated with alcohol than F. Scott Fizgerald and Ernest Hemingway. Fitzgerald, who gave the Jazz Age its moniker, will forever be associated with the speakeasy culture at once glamorized and criticized in *The Great Gatsby*. Hemingway, of course, did much to make the Mojito and Daiquiri the classic Caribbean drinks they are.

## DETECTIVE COCKTAILS

Cocktail culture saturates the detective novels of such genre-transcending writers as Raymond Chandler and Dashiell Hammett. In Chandler's *The Long Goodbye*, Philip Marlowe learns the mysteries of the Gimlet from doomed playboy Terry Lennox. Dashiell Hammett's Nick Charles is perhaps the greatest literary connoisseur of the cocktail; the hero of *The Thin Man* shares his love not only for Martinis but also for Bronx Cocktails and Knickerbockers.

Mojito

Bronx Cocktail

*Amaretto Sour Ball*

## ABSINTHE SOUR

2 oz absinthe

¾ oz lemon juice

1 oz simple syrup

Orange slice

Combine all ingredients but orange slice and shake well with ice. Strain into a sour glass and garnish with orange slice.

## AMARETTO SOUR BALL

1 oz amaretto

1 oz vodka

¾ oz lemon juice

1 oz simple syrup

Orange slice

Combine all ingredients but orange slice and shake well with ice. Strain into a sour glass and garnish with orange slice.

## APPLE BRANDY SOUR

2 oz apple brandy

¾ oz lemon juice

1 oz simple syrup

Orange slice

Combine all ingredients but orange slice and shake well with ice. Strain into a sour glass and garnish with orange slice.

## AMARETTO CHERRY SOUR

1 ½ oz amaretto

½ oz cherry brandy

¾ oz lemon juice

1 oz simple syrup

Orange slice

Combine all ingredients but orange slice and shake well with ice. Strain into a sour glass and garnish with orange slice.

## AMARETTO SWEET AND SOUR

1 ½ oz amaretto

½ oz Midori melon liqueur

¾ oz lemon juice

1 oz simple syrup

Orange slice

Combine all ingredients but orange slice and shake well with ice. Strain into a sour glass and garnish with orange slice.

## APPLE COCONUT SOUR

1 oz apple vodka

1 oz coconut rum

¾ oz lemon juice

1 oz simple syrup

Orange slice

Combine all ingredients but orange slice and shake well with ice. Strain into a sour glass and garnish with orange slice.

## AMARETTO SOUR

2 oz amaretto

¾ oz lemon juice

1 oz simple syrup

Orange slice

Combine all ingredients but orange slice and shake well with ice. Strain into a sour glass and garnish with orange slice.

## AMARETTO WHISKEY SOUR

1 oz amaretto

1 oz whiskey

¾ oz lemon juice

1 oz simple syrup

Orange slice

Combine all ingredients but orange slice and shake well with ice. Strain into a sour glass and garnish with orange slice.

## APPLEJACK SOUR

2 oz Applejack

¾ oz lemon juice

1 oz simple syrup

Orange slice

Combine all ingredients but orange slice and shake well with ice. Strain into a sour glass and garnish with orange slice.

## APPLE SOUR

2 oz apple vodka
¾ oz lemon juice
1 oz simple syrup
Orange slice

Combine all ingredients but orange slice and shake well with ice. Strain into a sour glass and garnish with orange slice.

## BELLAMY SCOTCH SOUR

2 oz Scotch whisky
¾ oz lemon juice
1 oz orange juice
¾ oz simple syrup
Pinch of powdered ginger
Orange slice

Combine all ingredients but orange slice and shake well with ice. Strain into a sour glass and garnish with orange slice.

## BOURBON STONE SOUR

2 oz Applejack
¾ oz lemon juice
1 oz simple syrup
1 oz orange juice
Orange slice

Combine all ingredients but orange slice and shake well with ice. Strain into a sour glass and garnish with orange slice.

## APRICOT BRANDY SOUR

2 oz apricot brandy
Splash of grenadine syrup
¾ oz lemon juice
1 oz simple syrup
Orange slice

Combine all ingredients but orange slice and shake well with ice. Strain into a sour glass and garnish with orange slice.

## BOSTON SOUR

2 oz bourbon
¾ oz lemon juice
1 oz simple syrup
1 egg white
Orange slice

Combine all ingredients but orange slice and shake well with ice. Strain into a sour glass and garnish with orange slice.

## BOURBON TRIPLE SOUR

1 oz bourbon
1 oz triple sec
¾ oz lemon juice
1 oz simple syrup
Orange slice

Combine all ingredients but orange slice and shake well with ice. Strain into a sour glass and garnish with orange slice.

## APRICOT SOUR

2 oz apricot brandy
¼ oz apricot nectar
¾ oz lemon juice
¾ oz simple syrup
Orange slice

Combine all ingredients but orange slice and shake well with ice. Strain into a sour glass and garnish with orange slice.

## BOURBON SOUR

2 oz bourbon
¾ oz lemon juice
1 oz simple syrup
Orange slice

Combine all ingredients but orange slice and shake well with ice. Strain into a sour glass and garnish with orange slice.

## BRANDY SOUR

2 oz brandy
¾ oz lemon juice
1 oz simple syrup
Orange slice

Combine all ingredients but orange slice and shake well with ice. Strain into a sour glass and garnish with orange slice.

Apricot Sour

Bourbon Triple Sour

Applejack Sour

Bourbon Stone Sour

Boston Sour

## CALIFORNIA SOUR

1 oz amaretto
1 oz coconut rum
¾ oz lemon juice
1 oz simple syrup
Orange slice

Combine all ingredients but orange slice and shake well with ice. Strain into a sour glass and garnish with orange slice.

## CANDY APPLE SOUR

2 oz apple brandy
1 oz grenadine syrup
¾ oz lemon juice
1 oz simple syrup
Orange slice

Combine all ingredients but orange slice and shake well with ice. Strain into a sour glass and garnish with orange slice.

## CAPE COD SOUR SQUISHY

1 oz light rum
½ oz sour apple schnapps
1 oz cranberry juice
¾ oz lemon juice
1 oz simple syrup
Orange slice

Combine all ingredients but orange slice and shake well with ice. Strain into a sour glass and garnish with orange slice.

## CHERRY SOUR

2 oz brandy
¾ oz lemon juice
1 oz simple syrup
3 maraschino cherries

Combine all ingredients but cherries and shake well with ice. Strain into a sour glass and garnish with cherries.

## CHAMBORD SOUR

2 oz Chambord
¾ oz lemon juice
1 oz simple syrup
Orange slice

Combine all ingredients but orange slice and shake well with ice. Strain into a sour glass and garnish with orange slice.

*Cherry Sour*

## CHERRY VODKA SOUR

1 ½ oz vodka
½ oz maraschino liqueur
¾ oz lemon juice
1 oz simple syrup
Orange slice

Combine all ingredients but orange slice and shake well with ice. Strain into a sour glass and garnish with orange slice.

## COFFEE SOUR

1 ½ oz brandy
½ oz Kahlúa
¾ oz lemon juice
1 oz simple syrup
Orange slice

Combine all ingredients but orange slice and shake well with ice. Strain into a sour glass and garnish with orange slice.

## CUBAN SOUR

2 oz gold rum
¾ oz lime juice
1 oz simple syrup
Orange slice

Combine all ingredients but orange slice and shake well with ice. Strain into a sour glass and garnish with orange slice.

*Cuban Sour*

## CYPRUS BRANDY SOUR

2 oz Cyprus brandy

¾ oz lemon juice

1 oz simple syrup

Orange slice

Combine all ingredients but orange slice and shake well with ice. Strain into a sour glass and garnish with orange slice.

## EASTERN SOUR

2 oz bourbon

¾ oz lime juice

1 ¼ oz orange juice

¼ oz orgeat syrup

¼ oz simple syrup

Orange slice

Combine all ingredients but orange slice and shake well with ice. Strain into a sour glass and garnish with orange slice.

## FIREMAN'S SOUR

2 oz light rum

¾ oz lime juice

½ oz grenadine syrup

1 oz simple syrup

Orange slice

Combine all ingredients but orange slice and shake well with ice. Strain into a sour glass and garnish with orange slice.

## DARK SOUR ALMOND

1 oz amaretto

1 oz Cointreau

¾ oz lemon juice

1 oz simple syrup

Orange slice

Combine all ingredients but orange slice and shake well with ice. Strain into a sour glass and garnish with orange slice.

## EGG SOUR

1 oz brandy

1 oz curaçao

¾ oz lemon juice

1 oz simple syrup

1 egg white

Orange slice

Combine all ingredients but orange slice and shake well with ice. Strain into a sour glass and garnish with orange slice.

## FRISCO SOUR

1 ½ oz bourbon

½ oz Bénédictine

¾ oz lemon juice

1 oz simple syrup

Orange slice

Combine all ingredients but orange slice and shake well with ice. Strain into a sour glass and garnish with orange slice.

## DOUBLE STANDARD SOUR

1 oz whiskey

1 oz gin

¾ oz lemon juice

1 oz simple syrup

Splash of grenadine syrup

Orange slice

Combine all ingredients but orange slice and shake well with ice. Strain into a sour glass and garnish with orange slice.

## FANCY SOUR

2 oz dry vermouth

¾ oz lemon juice

1 oz simple syrup

½ oz maraschino syrup

Orange slice

Combine all ingredients but orange slice and shake well with ice. Strain into a sour glass and garnish with orange slice.

## GIN SOUR

2 oz gin

¾ oz lemon juice

1 oz simple syrup

Orange slice

Combine all ingredients but orange slice and shake well with ice. Strain into a sour glass and garnish with orange slice.

*Eastern Sour*

## GRAND MARNIER SOUR

2 oz Grand Marnier
¾ oz lemon juice
1 oz simple syrup
Orange slice

Combine all ingredients but orange slice and shake well with ice. Strain into a sour glass and garnish with orange slice.

## IGP APRICOT SOUR

2 oz Inca Gold Pisco
½ oz apricot nectar
¾ oz lemon juice
1 oz simple syrup
Orange slice

Combine all ingredients but orange slice and shake well with ice. Strain into a sour glass and garnish with orange slice.

## JAMAICA SOUR

2 oz dark rum
¾ oz lemon juice
1 oz grenadine syrup
Orange slice

Combine all ingredients but orange slice and shake well with ice. Strain into a sour glass and garnish with orange slice.

## GT SOUR

1 ½ oz gin
1 ½ oz tonic water
¾ oz lemon juice
1 oz simple syrup
Lemon slice

Combine all ingredients but lemon slice and shake well with ice. Strain into a sour glass and garnish with lemon slice.

## JACK ROSE

1 ½ oz applejack
¾ oz lemon juice
1 oz simple syrup
2 dashes of grenadine
  syrup
Orange peel
Cherry

Combine all ingredients but fruit and shake well with ice. Strain into a sour glass and garnish with orange peel and cherry.

## KAHLÚA SOUR

2 oz Kahlúa
¾ oz lemon juice
1 oz simple syrup
Orange slice

Combine all ingredients but orange slice and shake well with ice. Strain into a sour glass and garnish with orange slice.

## HAWAIIAN STONE SOUR

2 oz whiskey
¾ oz lemon juice
1 oz simple syrup
1 ½ oz pineapple juice
Pineapple wedge

Combine all ingredients but pineapple wedge and shake well with ice. Strain into a sour glass and garnish with pineapple wedge.

## JACK SOUR

1 ½ oz Jack Daniel's
  Tennessee whiskey
¼ oz cherry liqueur
¾ oz lemon juice
1 oz simple syrup
Orange slice

Combine all ingredients but orange slice and shake well with ice. Strain into a sour glass and garnish with orange slice.

## LONDON SOUR

2 oz gin
¾ oz lemon juice
½ oz orgeat syrup
½ oz simple syrup
Orange slice

Combine all ingredients but orange slice and shake well with ice. Strain into a sour glass and garnish with orange slice.

*Jack Rose*

## LOVE GONE SOUR

1 oz Cognac
1 oz Alizé Red Passion
   liqueur
¾ oz lemon juice
1 oz simple syrup
Cherry

Combine all ingredients but cherry
and shake well with ice. Strain into a
sour glass and garnish with cherry.

## MACMELON SOUR

2 oz Midori melon liqueur
½ oz lime juice
½ oz lemon juice
1 oz simple syrup
Orange slice

Combine all ingredients but
orange slice and shake well with
ice. Strain into a sour glass and
garnish with orange slice.

## MANGO SOUR

2 oz pisco brandy
¾ oz lime juice
1 oz simple syrup
1 oz mango nectar
Orange slice

Combine all ingredients but
orange slice and shake well with
ice. Strain into a sour glass and
garnish with orange slice.

## MCWHISKEY SOUR

2 oz Irish whiskey
¾ oz lemon juice
1 oz simple syrup
Orange slice

Combine all ingredients but
orange slice and shake well with
ice. Strain into a sour glass and
garnish with orange slice.

## MELON SOUR

1 ½ oz Midori melon
   liqueur
½ oz Yellow Chartreuse
¾ oz lemon juice
1 oz simple syrup
Orange slice

Combine all ingredients but
orange slice and shake well with
ice. Strain into a sour glass and
garnish with orange slice.

## MISTY SOUR

2 oz Canadian Mist whiskey
¾ oz lemon juice
1 oz simple syrup
Orange slice

Combine all ingredients but
orange slice and shake well with
ice. Strain into a sour glass and
garnish with orange slice.

## MIDORI SOUR

2 oz Midori melon liqueur
¾ oz lemon juice
1 oz simple syrup
Orange slice

Combine all ingredients but
orange slice and shake well with
ice. Strain into a sour glass and
garnish with orange slice.

## MONTREAL GIN SOUR

2 oz gin
¾ oz lemon juice
1 oz simple syrup
½ egg white
Orange slice

Combine all ingredients but
orange slice and shake well with
ice. Strain into a sour glass and
garnish with orange slice.

## NEW YORK SOUR

2 oz gin
¾ oz lemon juice
1 oz simple syrup
Red wine
Orange slice

Combine gin, juice, and syrup
and shake well with ice. Strain
into a sour glass, top with a float
of red wine, and garnish with
orange slice.

*New York Sour*

*Pisco Sour*

## PISCO SOUR

2 oz pisco brandy
¾ oz lemon juice
1 oz simple syrup
Orange slice

Combine all ingredients but orange slice and shake well with ice. Strain into a sour glass and garnish with orange slice.

## PUERTO RICO SOUR

1 ½ oz light rum
½ oz banana liqueur
¾ oz lemon juice
1 oz simple syrup
Orange slice

Combine all ingredients but orange slice and shake well with ice. Strain into a sour glass and garnish with orange slice.

## ROYAL SOUR KISS

1 ½ oz Crown Royal Canadian whisky
½ oz sour apple schnapps
¾ oz lime juice
1 oz simple syrup
Orange slice

Combine all ingredients but orange slice and shake well with ice. Strain into a sour glass and garnish with orange slice.

## POTRERO SOUR

1 oz bourbon
½ oz apricot liqueur
½ oz dark rum
¾ oz lemon juice
1 oz simple syrup
1 egg white
Orange slice

Combine all ingredients but orange slice and shake well with ice. Strain into a sour glass and garnish with orange slice.

## RAINBOW SOUR

1 oz Pineau des Charentes
1 oz apricot brandy
¾ oz lemon juice
1 oz simple syrup
Orange slice

Combine all ingredients but orange slice and shake well with ice. Strain into a sour glass and garnish with orange slice.

## RUM SOUR

2 oz rum
¾ oz lemon juice
1 oz simple syrup
Orange slice

Combine all ingredients but orange slice and shake well with ice. Strain into a sour glass and garnish with orange slice.

## POWER SOUR

1 ½ oz bourbon
1 oz energy drink of choice
¾ oz lemon juice
½ oz simple syrup
Orange slice

Combine all ingredients but orange slice and shake well with ice. Strain into a sour glass and garnish with orange slice.

## RASPBERRY SOUR

1 ½ oz vodka
½ oz Grand Marnier
¾ oz lime juice
1 oz simple syrup
1 oz seedless raspberry puree

Combine all ingredients and shake well with ice. Strain into a sour glass.

## RYE SOUR

2 oz rye
¾ oz lemon juice
1 oz simple syrup
Orange slice

Combine all ingredients but orange slice and shake well with ice. Strain into a sour glass and garnish with orange slice.

## SCOTCH MELON SOUR

1 oz Scotch whisky
1 oz Midori melon liqueur
¾ oz lemon juice
1 oz simple syrup
Lemon twist

Combine all ingredients but lemon twist and shake well with ice. Strain into a sour glass and garnish with lemon twist.

## TEQUILA SOUR

2 oz tequila
¾ oz lemon juice
1 oz simple syrup
Orange slice

Combine all ingredients but orange slice and shake well with ice. Strain into a sour glass and garnish with orange slice.

## WARD EIGHT

2 oz bourbon
¾ oz lemon juice
1 oz simple syrup
¼ oz grenadine syrup
Orange slice
Cherry

Combine all ingredients but orange slice and cherry, and shake well with ice. Strain into a sour glass and garnish with orange slice and cherry.

## SCOTCH SOUR

2 oz Scotch whisky
¾ oz lemon juice
1 oz simple syrup
Orange slice

Combine all ingredients but orange slice and shake well with ice. Strain into a sour glass and garnish with orange slice.

## UK SOUR

1 ½ oz Scotch whisky
½ oz apricot liqueur
¾ oz lemon juice
½ oz cinnamon syrup
2 oz red wine
Orange slice

Combine all ingredients but orange slice and shake well with ice. Strain into a sour glass and garnish with orange slice.

## WHISKEY SOUR

2 oz whiskey of choice
¾ oz lemon juice
1 oz simple syrup
Orange slice

Combine all ingredients but orange slice and shake well with ice. Strain into a sour glass and garnish with orange slice.

## SHANDY SOUR

2 oz lager or ale
2 oz ginger beer
1 ounce orange curaçao
¾ oz lemon juice
1 oz simple syrup
Orange slice

Combine all ingredients but orange slice and shake well with ice. Strain into a sour glass and garnish with orange slice.

## VODKA SOUR

2 oz vodka
¾ oz lemon juice
1 oz simple syrup
Orange slice

Combine all ingredients but orange slice and shake well with ice. Strain into a sour glass and garnish with orange slice.

*Vodka Sour*

*Whiskey Sour*

## 1800 CRANBERRY TODDY

1 ½ oz 1800 Reposado tequila

½ oz triple sec

4 oz water, chilled

1 tsp demerara or powdered sugar

Lemon slice

Dissolve the sugar in 2 oz of the water. Add the tequila and triple sec along with the remaining water and stir. Garnish with lemon slice.

## BRANDY TODDY

2 oz brandy

4 oz water, chilled

1 tsp demerara or powdered sugar

Lemon slice

Dissolve the sugar in 2 oz of the water. Add the brandy and the remaining water and stir. Garnish with lemon slice.

## DANISH TODDY

1 ½ oz aquavit

½ oz cherry vodka

4 oz water, chilled

1 tsp demerara or powdered sugar

Lemon slice

Dissolve the sugar in 2 oz of the water. Add the aquavit and vodka and the remaining water and stir. Garnish with lemon slice.

## APPLEJACK TODDY

2 oz applejack

4 oz water, chilled

1 tsp demerara or powdered sugar

Grated nutmeg

Dissolve the sugar in 2 oz of the water. Add the applejack and the remaining water and stir. Dust with nutmeg.

## CANADIAN TODDY

2 oz Canadian whisky

4 oz water, chilled

1 tsp demerara or powdered sugar

Lemon slice

Dissolve the sugar in 2 oz of the water. Add the whisky and the remaining water and stir. Garnish with lemon slice.

## FRENCH TODDY

2 oz Cognac

4 oz water, chilled

1 tsp demerara or powdered sugar

Grated nutmeg

Dissolve the sugar in 2 oz of the water. Add the Cognac and the remaining water and stir. Dust with nutmeg.

## BOURBON TODDY

2 oz bourbon

4 oz water, chilled

1 tsp demerara or powdered sugar

Lemon slice

Dissolve the sugar in 2 oz of the water. Add the bourbon and the remaining water and stir. Garnish with lemon slice.

## CHAI TODDY

2 oz spiced rum

Dash of peppermint schnapps

4 oz water, chilled

1 tsp demerara or powdered sugar

Grated nutmeg

Dissolve the sugar in 2 oz of the water. Add the rum and schnapps and the remaining water and stir. Dust with nutmeg.

## GALLIANO TODDY

1 oz Scotch whisky

¾ oz Galliano

¼ oz grenadine syrup

4 oz water, chilled

1 tsp demerara or powdered sugar

Grated nutmeg

Dissolve the sugar in 2 oz of the water. Add the whisky, Galliano, syrup, and the remaining water and stir. Dust with nutmeg.

*Brandy Toddy*

## GIN TODDY

2 oz gin

4 oz water, chilled

1 tsp demerara or
   powdered sugar

Lemon slice

Dissolve the sugar in 2 oz of
the water. Add the gin and the
remaining water and stir. Garnish
with lemon slice.

## JERSEY TODDY

2 oz apple brandy

4 oz water, chilled

1 tsp demerara or
   powdered sugar

3 dashes of Angostura
   bitters

Lemon slice

Dissolve the sugar in 2 oz of the
water. Add the apple brandy,
bitters, and the remaining water
and stir. Garnish with lemon slice.

## RUM STONE TODDY

2 oz gold rum

4 oz orange juice, chilled

½ tsp demerara sugar

Grated nutmeg

Dissolve the sugar in 2 oz of
the juice. Add the rum and the
remaining juice and stir. Dust
with nutmeg.

## GRAND MARNIER TODDY

2 oz Grand Marnier

4 oz water, chilled

1 tsp demerara or
   powdered sugar

Grated nutmeg

Dissolve the sugar in 2 oz of the
water. Add the Grand Marnier and
the remaining water and stir. Dust
with nutmeg.

## RACETRACK TODDY

1 ½ oz gold rum

½ oz orange curaçao

4 oz water, chilled

1 tsp demerara or
   powdered sugar

Grated nutmeg

Dissolve the sugar in 2 oz of the
water. Add the rum and Curaçao
and the remaining water and stir.
Dust with nutmeg.

## RUM TODDY

2 oz dark rum

4 oz water, chilled

1 tsp demerara sugar

Grated nutmeg

Dissolve the sugar in 2 oz of
the water. Add the rum and the
remaining water and stir. Dust
with nutmeg.

## JAMAICAN TODDY

1 oz dark rum

½ oz triple sec

½ oz banana liqueur

4 oz water, chilled

1 tsp demerara sugar

Grated nutmeg

Dissolve the sugar in 2 oz of the
water. Add the rum, triple sec,
banana liqueur and the remaining
water and stir. Dust with nutmeg.

## ROCK-AND-RYE TODDY

2 oz Rock and Rye liqueur

2 dashes of Angostura
   bitters

4 oz water, chilled

1 tsp demerara or
   powdered sugar

Grated nutmeg

Dissolve the sugar in 2 oz of the
water. Add the Rock and Rye,
bitters, and the remaining water
and stir. Dust with nutmeg.

## SCOTCH TODDY

2 oz Scotch whisky

4 oz water, chilled

1 tsp demerara or
   powdered sugar

Lemon slice

Dissolve the sugar in 2 oz of the
water. Add the whisky and the
remaining water and stir. Garnish
with lemon slice.

*Scotch Toddy*

*Strega Toddy*

## STREGA TODDY

1 oz Strega liqueur

¾ oz brandy

4 oz water, chilled

1 tsp demerara or
   powdered sugar

Grated nutmeg

Dissolve the sugar in 2 oz of the
water. Add the Strega and brandy
and the remaining water and stir.
Dust with nutmeg.

## TEA TODDY

2 oz bourbon

4 oz iced tea

1 tsp demerara or
   powdered sugar

Lemon slice

Dissolve the sugar in 2 oz of the
tea. Add the bourbon and the
remaining tea and stir. Garnish
with lemon slice.

*Tea Toddy*

*Black Russian*

*Caipirinha*

## AGGRAVATION

1 ½ oz Scotch whisky
½ oz Kahlúa
½ oz milk or half-and-half

Combine whisky and Kahlúa in an old-fashioned glass over ice and stir. Top with a float of milk or half-and-half.

## BANSHEE

1 oz crème de banane
1 oz white crème de cacao
2 oz heavy cream

Combine all ingredients and shake well with ice. Strain into a rocks glass over ice. Can also be served without ice as an "up" drink.

## BRAVE BULL

1 oz tequila
1 oz Kahlúa

Combine over ice in an old-fashioned glass. No garnish.

## AMBER DREAM

2 oz gin
1 oz dry vermouth
¼ oz Yellow Chartreuse
Dash of bitters
Orange peel

Combine gin, vermouth, Chartreuse, and bitters over ice in an old-fashioned glass. Garnish with orange peel.

## BLACK ROSE

2 oz bourbon
1 dash of grenadine syrup
2 dashes of bitters
Lemon peel

In an old-fashioned glass mostly filled with ice, combine bourbon, grenadine, and bitters and stir. Garnish with lemon peel.

## CAIPIRINHA

2 oz cachaça
1 tsp brown sugar
½ lime, quartered

Muddle the lime quarters with the sugar in the bottom of a mixing glass. Add the cachaça and shake well. Pour all contents into a rocks glass.

## AMERICANO

¾ oz Campari
¾ oz sweet vermouth
Club soda
Lemon peel

Combine Campari and vermouth over ice in a rocks glass and top with a splash of soda. Garnish with lemon peel.

## BLACK RUSSIAN

1 oz vodka
1 oz Kahlúa

Combine over ice in an old-fashioned glass. No garnish.

## CAIPIRINHA DE UVA

2 oz cachaça
1 tsp brown sugar
½ lime, quartered
4 seedless green grapes

Muddle the lime quarters and grapes with the sugar in the bottom of a mixing glass. Add the cachaça and shake well. Pour all contents into a rocks glass.

## CAIPIROSCA

2 oz vodka

1 tsp brown sugar

½ lime, quartered

Muddle the lime quarters with the sugar in the bottom of a mixing glass. Add the vodka and shake well. Pour all contents into a rocks glass.

## COLORADO BULLDOG

1 oz Kahlúa

2 oz chilled milk

2 oz cola

Combine the Kahlúa and milk in an old-fashioned glass. Gently stir in the cola to fill the glass.

## DIRTY WHITE MOTHER

1 ½ oz brandy

1 oz Kahlúa

1 ½ oz heavy cream

Combine all the ingredients and shake with ice. Strain into a rocks glass over ice.

## CHERRY CAIPIRINHA

2 oz cachaça

1 tsp brown sugar

½ lime, quartered

4 pitted cherries (sweet or sour)

Muddle the lime quarters and cherries with the sugar in the bottom of a mixing glass. Add the cachaça and shake well. Pour all contents into a rocks glass.

## DIRTY BIRD

1 oz bourbon

1 oz tequila

½ oz lime juice

½ oz lemon juice

1 oz simple syrup

Lemon peel

In the bottom of a rocks glass, dissolve the syrup in the juices. Fill the glass with ice, add the whiskey and tequila, and stir. Garnish with lemon peel.

## FRENCH KISS

2 oz sweet vermouth

2 oz dry vermouth

Lemon peel

Combine vermouths over ice in a white wine glass. Garnish with lemon peel.

## CLAREMONT

1 ½ oz bourbon

¾ oz orange Curaçao

2 orange slices

2 cherries (sweet or sour)

2 dashes of Angostura bitters

1 oz club soda

In the bottom of an old-fashioned glass, muddle the bitters, curaçao, and one each of the cherries and orange slices. Remove the muddled orange slice and add the bourbon, some ice, and the soda. Garnish with remaining orange slice and cherry.

## DIRTY MOTHER

1 ½ oz brandy

1 oz Kahlúa

Combine over ice in a rocks glass.

## GODFATHER

1 oz Scotch whisky

1 oz Amaretto

Combine over ice in a rocks glass.

*Caipirosca*

## ICEBERG

2 oz lemon vodka

3 dashes Pernod

Use the Pernod to coat the interior of an empty old-fashioned glass, and discard extra. Add ice and then vodka, and stir.

## MAI TAI

2 oz dark rum

¾ oz Curaçao

¾ oz fresh lime juice

¼ oz orgeat syrup

Mint sprig

Lime wedge

Shake rum, Curaçao, lime juice, and syrup with ice and strain into an ice-filled old-fashioned glass. Garnish with mint and lime.

## MUDSLIDE

1 oz vodka

1 oz Kahlúa

1 oz Bailey's Irish Cream

1 oz cream

Shake all the ingredients with ice and strain into a rocks glass over ice.

## KENTUCKY COLONEL

2 oz bourbon

1 oz Bénédictine

Combine bourbon and Bénédictine and shake with ice. Strain into a rocks glass filled with crushed ice.

## MAN O' WAR

1 ½ oz bourbon

1 oz Curaçao

½ oz sweet vermouth

½ oz orange juice

Orange slice

Shake all ingredients but the orange with ice and strain into an ice-filled old-fashioned glass. Garnish with orange slice.

## NEGRONI

1 oz Campari

1 oz sweet vermouth

1 oz gin

Orange peel for garnish

Combine all ingredients in an iced old-fashioned glass and stir. Garnish with orange peel. If you substitute Carpano for the Campari and add an extra splash of gin, the resulting drink is a Buñueloni, a favorite of the great filmmaker Luis Buñuel.

## LATIN LOVER

1 oz coconut rum

1 oz banana rum

1 oz Coco Lopez

3 oz pineapple juice

1 oz raspberry juice

1 oz cream

1 scoop of ice

Combine all ingredients in a blender and blend until smooth. Rim a hurricane glass with grenadine and shaved coconut. Pour the mixture into the hurricane glass.

## MARLENE DIETRICH

2 oz Canadian whisky

½ oz curaçao

3 dashes of of Angostura bitters

1 piece lemon

1 piece orange

Combine the whisky, curaçao, and bitters and shake with ice. Strain into an ice-filled rocks glass. Squeeze in the lemon and orange.

## NUTS AND BERRIES

½ oz Frangelico liqueur

½ oz Chambord

2 oz cream

Shake all ingredients with ice and strain into a chilled old-fashioned glass.

*Mai Tai*

*Negroni*

## NUTTY IRISHMAN

1 oz Bailey's Irish Cream
1 oz Frangelico

Shake with ice and strain over ice in a rocks glass.

## PEPPERMINT PATTY

1 oz crème de menthe
1 oz light crème de cacao

Combine ingredients over ice in a rocks glass and stir.

## ROASTED TOASTED ALMOND

1 ½ oz Grand Marnier
1 ½ oz Kahlúa
1 ½ oz Bailey's Irish Cream

Shake all three liqueurs with ice and strain into an old-fashioned glass over ice.

## OLD FASHIONED

2 oz bourbon
1 tsp superfine sugar
2 dashes of Angostura bitters
2 orange slices
2 maraschino cherries
Club soda (or plain water)

In the bottom of an old-fashioned glass, muddle one each of the orange slices and cherries with the sugar, the bitters, and a splash of soda. Remove the muddled orange and add the bourbon, some ice, and soda. Garnish with remaining orange slice and cherry.

## PINK MAI TAI

1 oz dark rum
1 oz light rum
1 oz orange Curaçao
½ oz lime juice
Dash of orgeat syrup
Dash of simple syrup
Dash of grenadine syrup
Pineapple wedge
Maraschino cherry

Build the drink over ice in an old-fashioned glass, in order. Garnish with pineapple wedge and cherry.

## RUSTY NAIL

2 oz Scotch whisky
¾ oz Drambuie liqueur

Pour the whisky over ice in an old-fashioned glass and float the Drambuie on top.

## PEARL HARBOR

1 oz vodka
½ oz Midori melon liqueur
4 oz pineapple juice

Combine ingredients over ice in a rocks glass and stir.

## PRAIRIE OYSTER (NON-ALCOHOLIC)

Dash of malt vinegar
Yolk of one egg
½ tsp Worcestershire sauce
½ tsp tomato ketchup
2 dashes of Tabasco sauce

Combine all ingredients in the order listed in an old-fashioned or shot glass. Drink in one gulp if possible.

## SAN SALVADOR

1 ½ oz dark rum
1 oz Curaçao
½ oz lime juice
1 ½ oz orange juice
Orange slice
Lime slice

Combine the rum, Curaçao, and juices and shake with ice. Strain into an old-fashioned glass over ice. Garnish with orange and lime slices.

*Old Fashioned*

*Rusty Nail*

## SAZERAC

2 oz Cognac

Splash of Ricard or Herbsaint

½ oz simple syrup

2 dashes of Peychaud's bitters

2 dashes of Angostura bitters

Lemon peel

Coat the inside of a rocks glass with the Ricard or Herbsaint and discard the remainder. Add the Cognac, syrup, and bitters and stir with ice cubes to chill. Strain into a chilled rocks glass and garnish with lemon peel.

## SCORPION

1 oz rum

1 oz brandy

¾ oz lemon juice

½ oz simple syrup

½ oz orgeat syrup

1 oz orange juice

2 pineapple wedges

2 cherries

Bruise a pineapple wedge and a cherry in a glass. Add the rum, brandy, juices and syrup and shake well. Strain into an old-fashioned glass over ice. Garnish with remaining pineapple and cherry.

## SIDECAR

1 oz brandy

1 oz Cointreau

¾ oz lemon juice

Orange peel

Combine the brandy, Cointreau, and lemon juice and shake with ice. Strain into an iced old-fashioned glass. Garnish with orange peel.

## SOMBRERO

1 ½ oz coffee brandy

1 oz light cream

Pour brandy over ice in an old-fashioned glass. Float cream on top.

## STONE FENCE

1 ½ oz bourbon

4 oz apple cider

½ oz lemon juice

Apple slice

Cherry

Combine bourbon, cider, and juice in a tumbler with ice. Garnish with the apple slice and cherry.

## SUFFERING BASTARD

1 ½ oz gold rum

1 oz overproof rum

¾ oz orange Curaçao

½ oz orgeat syrup

1 oz lime juice

2 oz orange juice

Lime slice

Orange slice

Shake the rums, Curaçao, juices and syrup and strain into a double old-fashioned glass over ice. Garnish with lime and orange slices.

## TOASTED ALMOND

1 oz Amaretto

1 oz Kahlúa

2 ½ oz cream

Combine all ingredients, shake with ice, and strain into an old-fashioned glass over ice. Can also be served "up."

*Freshly sliced orange*

Sazerac

*Suffering Bastard*

## STINGER

2 oz Cognac or brandy

1 oz white crème de menthe

Shake both ingredients with ice and strain into an old-fashioned glass filled with cracked ice.

## VODKA STINGER

1 ½ oz vodka

¾ oz white crème de menthe

Shake ingredients with ice and strain into a rocks glass filled with ice.

## WHITE RUSSIAN

1 oz vodka

1 oz Kahlúa

1 oz heavy cream

Shake ingredients with ice and strain into an old-fashioned glass.

*White Russian*

# U P
# DRINKS

AN UP DRINK IS THE CLASSIC IMAGE OF A COCKTAIL:
SHAKEN OR STIRRED WITH ICE AND SERVED, ALMOST
ALWAYS STRAINED, IN A COCKTAIL GLASS. UP DRINKS
ARE THE MOST ELEGANT OF THE COCKTAILS, AND NOT
ONLY BECAUSE OF THEIR PRESENTATION. SUBTLE OR
INTENSE, AUSTERE OR RICH, THEY TEND TO HAVE
DISTINCT PERSONALITIES.

# HOLLYWOOD COCKTAILS

## MARTINIS ON SCREEN

The most famous of all movie cocktails is, of course, James Bond's vodka martini—shaken, not stirred—but the martini as a mark of style and sophistication owes more to the decades-earlier classic comedies of the 1930s, notably the Thin Man movies.

Whiskey cocktails inherited the mantle of manliness passed on from classic Westerns, but other cocktails were seen as more feminine: when Rick, Humphrey Bogart's lovelorn hero in *Casablanca*, says "Here's looking at you, kid" to Ingrid Bergman's Ilsa, he has just mixed her a champagne cocktail (page 310).

"Softer" drinks in the hands of male characters came to suggest a lack of grit—as when the feckless Fredo orders a banana daiquiri in *The Godfather Part II*.

Next to martinis, no drink has exercised such a spell over Hollywood as the Manhattan (page 248). In *Some Like It Hot*, Marilyn Monroe's alluring Sugar Kane Kowalczyk imbibes Manhattans. Off screen, the Manhattan became the signature drink of Frank Sinatra's notorious Rat Pack.

Dry Martini

White Russian

## AGAVE MARGARITA

1 ½ oz tequila
1 oz agave syrup
1 oz lime juice
¾ oz water

Combine all ingredients in a mixer with ice and shake well. Strain into a chilled margarita or cocktail glass with a salted rim (salt rim by rubbing with lime and dipping in coarse salt).

## BARTENDER'S MARGARITA

1 ½ oz tequila
1 splash of cranberry juice
¾ oz triple sec
½ oz Grand Marnier
¾ oz lime juice
1 oz simple syrup

Combine all ingredients but Grand Marnier in a mixer with ice and shake well. Strain into a chilled margarita or cocktail glass and top with a float of Grand Marnier.

## BLACKJACK MARGARITA

1 ½ oz tequila
½ oz triple sec
½ oz Chambord
4 oz lime juice

Combine all ingredients in a mixer with ice and shake well. Strain into a chilled margarita or cocktail glass.

## APPLE PIE MARGARITA

½ oz tequila
½ oz sour apple schnapps
1 ½ oz apple juice
½ oz lime juice
½ oz simple syrup

Combine all ingredients in a mixer with ice and shake well. Strain into a chilled margarita or cocktail glass.

## BIG APPLE MARGARITA

2 oz tequila
1 oz Brentzen's Apple Liqueur
¾ oz lemon or lime juice
Green apple slice

Combine all ingredients but apple slice in a mixer with ice and shake well. Strain into a chilled margarita or cocktail glass. Garnish with apple slice.

## BLOOD ORANGE MARGARITA

1 ½ oz tequila
½ oz triple sec
2 oz blood orange juice
1 oz simple syrup
¾ oz lime juice

Combine all ingredients in a mixer with ice and shake well. Strain into a chilled margarita or cocktail glass.

## BANANA MARGARITA

1 oz tequila
1 oz crème de banane
½ oz triple sec
¾ oz lime juice
About ¼ of a banana, mashed

Combine all ingredients in a mixer with ice and shake well. Strain into a chilled margarita or cocktail glass.

## BLACK CHERRY MARGARITA

¾ oz black cherry schnapps
½ oz tequila
½ oz triple sec
2 oz orange juice
1 oz simple syrup
¾ oz lemon juice
8 oz crushed ice

Combine all ingredients in a blender and blend to desired consistency. Serve in a margarita or cocktail glass.

## BLOODY MARGARITA

1 ½ oz tequila
¾ oz Cointreau
1 oz blood orange juice
½ oz lime juice

Combine all ingredients in a mixer with ice and shake well. Strain into a chilled margarita or cocktail glass.

**Agave Margarita**

## BLUE LAGOON MARGARITA

1 ½ oz tequila
¾ oz Blue Curaçao
1 oz pineapple juice
½ oz lime juice
½ oz lemon-lime soda

Combine all ingredients in a mixer with ice and shake well. Strain into a chilled margarita or cocktail glass.

## CAPTAIN MARGARITA

1 ½ oz tequila
¾ oz Captain Morgan Lime Bite Rum
¾ oz lime juice
1 oz grenadine syrup

Combine all ingredients in a mixer with ice and shake well. Strain into a chilled margarita or cocktail glass.

## CHAMBORD MARGARITA

1 ½ oz tequila
¾ oz Cointreau
¾ oz Chambord
1 oz simple syrup
¾ oz lime juice

Combine all ingredients in a mixer with ice and shake well. Strain into a chilled margarita or cocktail glass.

## BLUSHING MARGARITA

1 ½ oz tequila
1 oz Cointreau
1 oz cranberry juice
½ oz lime juice

Combine all ingredients in a mixer with ice and shake well. Strain into a chilled margarita or cocktail glass.

## CASA NOBLE MARGARITA

2 oz Casa Noble Reposado tequila
½ oz Grand Marnier
1 oz lime juice

Combine all ingredients in a mixer with ice and shake well. Strain into a chilled margarita or cocktail glass.

## CHILI MARGARITA

2 oz tequila
1 oz pineapple juice
½ oz lemon juice
½ oz lime juice
1 oz simple syrup
1 small jalapeño pepper

Muddle half the pepper with the lime juice and syrup in the bottom of a mixing glass. Add the tequila and other juices and shake well with ice. Strain into a chilled margarita or cocktail glass and garnish with a twist made of the remaining half-pepper.

## CADILLAC MARGARITA

1 ½ oz tequila
1 oz Grand Marnier
¾ oz lime juice

Combine all ingredients in a mixer with ice and shake well. Strain into a chilled margarita or cocktail glass.

## CATALINA MARGARITA

1 ½ oz tequila
1 oz Blue Curaçao
1 oz peach schnapps
¾ oz lime juice
1 oz simple syrup

Combine all ingredients in a mixer with ice and shake well. Strain into a chilled margarita or cocktail glass.

## CLASSIC MARGARITA

1 ½ oz tequila
1 oz Cointreau
¾ oz lime juice

Combine all ingredients in a mixer with ice and shake well. Strain into a chilled margarita or cocktail glass with a salted rim (to salt the rim, moisten it with a piece of lime and dip the outside of the rim in coarse salt).

Blue Lagoon Margarita

Classic Margarita

Cranberry Margarita

## CRANBERRY MARGARITA

1 ½ oz tequila

1 oz Cointreau

1 oz cranberry juice

¾ oz lime juice

¾ oz simple syrup

Combine all ingredients in a mixer with ice and shake well. Strain into a chilled margarita or cocktail glass.

## DIXIE MARGARITA

1 ½ oz pecan praline liqueur

½ oz Cointreau

1 oz lime juice

Combine all ingredients in a mixer with ice and shake well. Strain into a chilled margarita or cocktail glass.

## GALA MARGARITA

1 ½ oz tequila

1 oz Gran Gala orange liqueur

1 oz lime juice

Combine all ingredients in a mixer with ice and shake well. Strain into a chilled margarita or cocktail glass.

## CREAMSICLE MARGARITA

1 ½ oz tequila

1 oz Grand Marnier

1 oz coconut water

1 oz canned light coconut milk

1 oz simple syrup

¾ oz lime juice

Combine all ingredients in a mixer with ice and shake well. Strain into a chilled margarita or cocktail glass.

## ELECTRIC MARGARITA

1 ½ oz tequila

½ oz Blue Curaçao

¾ oz lime juice

Combine all ingredients in a mixer with ice and shake well. Strain into a chilled margarita or cocktail glass with a salted rim.

## GOLDEN GRAND MARGARITA

1 ½ oz gold tequila

1 oz Grand Marnier

¾ oz lime juice

Combine all ingredients in a mixer with ice and shake well. Strain into a chilled margarita or cocktail glass

## CUERVO GOLDEN MARGARITA

1 ½ oz Cuervo Gold tequila

1 oz Cointreau

2 oz orange juice

¾ oz lime juice

Combine all ingredients in a mixer with ice and shake well. Strain into a chilled margarita or cocktail glass.

## FRISCO MARGARITA

1 ½ oz tequila

½ oz Bénédictine

¾ oz lemon juice

Combine all ingredients in a mixer with ice and shake well. Strain into a chilled margarita or cocktail glass.

## GOLDEN MARGARITA

1 ½ oz gold tequila

½ oz Grand Marnier

½ oz Cointreau

¾ oz lime juice

Combine all ingredients in a mixer with ice and shake well. Strain into a chilled margarita or cocktail glass.

## GREEN APPLE MARGARITA

1 ½ oz tequila
1 oz sour apple schnapps
¾ oz lime juice
1 oz simple syrup

Combine all ingredients in a mixer with ice and shake well. Strain into a chilled margarita or cocktail glass.

## HAWAIIAN MARGARITA

1 ½ oz tequila
1 oz Blue Curaçao
¼ oz coconut liqueur
1 oz pineapple juice
¾ oz lime juice

Combine all ingredients in a mixer with ice and shake well. Strain into a chilled margarita or cocktail glass.

## JALISCO MARGARITA

2 oz gold tequila
½ oz triple sec
1 oz lime juice

Combine all ingredients in a mixer with ice and shake well. Strain into a chilled margarita or cocktail glass.

## GREEN IGUANA MARGARITA

1 ½ oz tequila
1 oz Midori melon liqueur
¾ oz lime juice

Combine all ingredients in a mixer with ice and shake well. Strain into a chilled margarita or cocktail glass.

## HIGHLAND MARGARITA

1 ½ oz tequila
½ oz Cointreau
½ oz Drambuie
¾ oz lime juice
1 oz simple syrup

Combine all ingredients in a mixer with ice and shake well. Strain into a chilled margarita or cocktail glass.

## KAMIKAZE MARGARITA

1 oz vodka
1 oz tequila
¾ oz triple sec
1 oz lime juice
¾ oz simple syrup

Combine all ingredients in a mixer with ice and shake well. Strain into a chilled margarita or cocktail glass.

## GYPSY MARGARITA

1 oz vodka
⅓ oz tequila
⅓ oz Cointreau
⅓ oz crème de cassis
¾ oz lime juice

Combine all ingredients in a mixer with ice and shake well. Strain into a chilled margarita or cocktail glass.

## ITALIAN MARGARITA

1 ½ oz tequila
½ oz Cointreau
½ oz amaretto
¾ oz lime juice

Combine all ingredients in a mixer with ice and shake well. Strain into a chilled margarita or cocktail glass.

## MAMBO MARGARITA

1 oz white tequila
1 oz light rum
¾ oz triple sec
¾ oz lime juice

Combine all ingredients in a mixer with ice and shake well. Strain into a chilled margarita or cocktail glass.

*Green Apple Margarita*

Mile High Margarita

## MANGO MARGARITA

1 ½ oz tequila

½ oz triple sec

¾ oz mango nectar

¾ oz lime juice

Combine all ingredients in a mixer with ice and shake well. Strain into a chilled margarita or cocktail glass.

## MELIORA MARGARITA

1 ½ oz tequila

1 oz Cointreau

¾ oz grapefruit juice

½ oz lime juice

Combine all ingredients in a mixer with ice and shake well. Strain into a chilled margarita or cocktail glass with a salted rim.

## MIDORI MARGARITA

1 oz tequila

1 oz Midori melon liqueur

¾ oz lime juice

Combine all ingredients in a mixer with ice and shake well. Strain into a chilled margarita or cocktail glass.

## MARGARITA LITE

1 ½ oz tequila

1 oz Cointreau

½ oz lime juice

1 oz tonic water

Combine all ingredients except tonic water in a mixer with ice and shake well. Strain into a chilled margarita or cocktail glass and top with tonic water.

## MELON MARGARITA

1 oz tequila

1 oz Midori melon liqueur

¼ oz Galliano

1 oz lime juice

½ oz simple syrup

Combine all ingredients in a mixer with ice and shake well. Strain into a chilled margarita or cocktail glass.

## MILE HIGH MARGARITA

1 ½ oz tequila

1 oz Grand Marnier

¾ oz lime juice

½ oz raspberry syrup

Combine all ingredients in a mixer with ice and shake well. Strain into a chilled margarita or cocktail glass

## MAYBACH MARGARITA

2 oz tequila

¾ oz Grand Marnier

¾ oz lime juice

1 oz simple syrup

½ oz orange juice

Combine all ingredients in a mixer with ice and shake well. Strain into a chilled margarita or cocktail glass.

## MEXICO CITY MARGARITA

1 ½ oz tequila

1 oz triple sec

½ oz lime juice

½ oz pureed zapote chico fruit

Combine all ingredients in a mixer with ice and shake well. Strain into a chilled margarita or cocktail glass.

## OC MARGARITA

1 ½ oz tequila

¾ oz Grand Marnier

½ oz triple sec

¾ oz lime juice

1 oz simple syrup

Combine all ingredients in a mixer with ice and shake well. Strain into a chilled margarita or cocktail glass with a salted rim.

## ORANGE MARGARITA

1 ½ oz tequila
1 oz triple sec
2 oz orange juice
½ oz lime juice

Combine all ingredients in a mixer with ice and shake well. Strain into a chilled margarita or cocktail glass.

## PEACH MARGARITA

1 ½ oz tequila
1 oz peach schnapps
¾ oz lime juice
¾ oz simple syrup
Dash of grenadine syrup

Combine all ingredients in a mixer with ice and shake well. Strain into a chilled margarita or cocktail glass.

## PLATINUM GRAND MARGARITA

1 ½ oz tequila
1 oz Cointreau
¼ oz Irish Mist liqueur
¾ oz lime juice

Combine all ingredients in a mixer with ice and shake well. Strain into a chilled margarita or cocktail glass.

## PARTIDA MARGARITA

1 ½ oz Partida white tequila
¾ oz spring water
¾ oz lime juice
¾ oz Partida agave nectar

Combine all ingredients in a mixer with ice and shake well. Strain into a chilled margarita or cocktail glass.

## PEAR MARGARITA

1 ½ oz tequila
½ oz triple sec
½ oz pear liqueur
¾ oz lime juice
1 oz simple syrup

Combine all ingredients in a mixer with ice and shake well. Strain into a chilled margarita or cocktail glass.

## PRESIDENTIAL MARGARITA

1 ½ oz tequila
½ oz Cointreau
½ oz Presidente brandy
¾ oz lime juice

Combine all ingredients in a mixer with ice and shake well. Strain into a chilled margarita or cocktail glass.

## PASSION MARGARITA

¾ oz tequila
¾ oz Alizé Gold
1 oz triple sec
½ oz lime juice
½ oz orange or tangerine juice

Combine all ingredients in a mixer with ice and shake well. Strain into a chilled margarita or cocktail glass with a salted rim.

## PIRATE MARGARITA

1 ¼ oz coconut rum
¾ oz amaretto
¾ oz triple sec
2 oz orange juice
¼ oz heavy cream

Combine all ingredients in a mixer with ice and shake well. Strain into a chilled margarita or cocktail glass.

## PURPLE MARGARITA

1 ½ oz tequila
1 oz Chambord
¾ oz lime juice
¾ oz cranberry juice
1 oz simple syrup

Combine all ingredients in a mixer with ice and shake well. Strain into a chilled margarita or cocktail glass.

Pear Margarita

## SANGRIA MARGARITA

1 ½ oz tequila

1 oz triple sec

½ oz lime juice

1 oz sangria

Combine all ingredients in a mixer with ice and shake well. Strain into a chilled margarita or cocktail glass.

## SPICY MARGARITA

1 ½ oz tequila

1 oz Cointreau

¾ oz lime juice

1 serrano pepper

Combine all ingredients but pepper in a mixer with ice and shake well. Strain into a chilled margarita or cocktail glass rimmed with serrano pepper.

## STRAWBERRY MARGARITA

1 oz tequila

½ oz triple sec

½ oz strawberry schnapps

¾ oz lemon juice

3 strawberries, leaves removed

Crushed ice

Combine all ingredients in a mixer with ice and shake well. Pour into a chilled margarita or cocktail glass with a salted rim.

## SMOKED MARGARITA

1 ½ oz tequila

1 oz triple sec

¾ oz lime juice

3 drops of Cholula hot sauce

Combine all ingredients in a mixer with ice and shake well. Strain into a chilled margarita or cocktail glass.

## STRAWBERRY MANGO MARGARITA

1 ½ oz tequila

1 oz triple sec

1 oz mango nectar

¾ oz lime juice

4-5 strawberries, leaves removed

Crushed ice

Combine all ingredients in a blender and blend until smooth. Pour into a chilled margarita or cocktail glass.

## TANGERINE MARGARITA

2 oz tequila

1 oz Cointreau

½ oz lime juice

½ oz tangerine juice

Combine all ingredients in a mixer with ice and shake well. Pour over ice in a chilled margarita or cocktail glass with a salted rim.

## SOUR APPLE MARGARITA

1 ½ oz tequila

1 oz sour apple schnapps

¾ oz lemon juice

½ oz simple syrup

Combine all ingredients in a mixer with ice and shake well. Strain into a chilled margarita or cocktail glass.

*Washed strawberries in a bowl*

*Strawberry Margarita*

### TENNESSEE MARGARITA

1 oz Tennessee whiskey

½ oz Grand Marnier

¾ oz lime juice

Combine all ingredients in a mixer with ice and shake well. Pour over ice in a chilled margarita or rocks glass.

### WATERMELON MARGARITA

1 ½ oz tequila

1 oz triple sec

¾ oz lime juice

1 oz simple syrup

2 wedges watermelon, rinds removed

Combine all ingredients in blender and blend until smooth. Pour into a chilled margarita or cocktail glass with a salted rim.

### WHITECAP MARGARITA

2 oz white tequila

1 oz Coco Lopez

½ oz lime juice

Combine all ingredients in a mixer with ice and shake well. Pour over ice in a chilled margarita or cocktail glass with a salted rim.

*Fresh coconut*

*Whitecap Margarita*

## 24 KARROT MARTINI

2 ½ oz vodka

Spicy baby carrot

Shake vodka with ice and strain into a chilled cocktail glass. Garnish with the carrot.

## ALIZÉ TROPICAL MARTINI

2 oz Alizé Gold Passion

½ oz Malibu

Maraschino cherry

Shake Alizé and Malibu with ice and strain into a chilled cocktail glass. Garnish with cherry.

## ANGEL MARTINI

1 ½ oz vodka

½ oz Frangelico

Shake with ice and strain into a chilled cocktail glass.

## AFFINITY MARTINI

1 oz Scotch

1 oz sweet vermouth

1 oz dry vermouth

2 dashes of Angostura bitters

Maraschino cherry

Shake Scotch, vermouths, and bitters with ice and strain into a chilled cocktail glass. Garnish with the cherry.

## ALOHA MARTINI

2 oz vodka

¼ oz apricot brandy

¼ oz pineapple juice

Pineapple wedge

Shake vodka, brandy, and juice with ice and strain into a chilled cocktail glass. Garnish with pineapple wedge.

## ANTINI MARTINI

2 oz vodka

½ oz Lillet rouge

Orange peel

Shake vodka and Lillet with ice and strain into a chilled cocktail glass. Garnish with orange peel.

## ALIZÉ MARTINI

1 ½ oz Alizé Gold Passion

½ oz vodka

Lemon slice

Shake Alizé and vodka with ice and strain into a chilled cocktail glass. Garnish with lemon slice.

*Maraschino cherries*

Affinity Martini

## APRICOT MARTINI

1 oz vodka

1 oz apricot brandy

1 oz chocolate liqueur

Maraschino cherry

Shake vodka, brandy, and liqueur with ice and strain into a chilled cocktail glass. Garnish with cherry.

## ATTY MARTINI

2 oz gin

½ oz extra dry vermouth

2 dashes of crème de violette

Lemon peel

Shake gin, vermouth, and crème de violette with ice and strain into a chilled cocktail glass. Garnish with lemon peel.

## BACARDI SWEET MARTINI

2 oz Bacardi white rum

2 oz sweet vermouth

Orange peel

Shake rum and vermouth with ice and strain into a chilled cocktail glass. Garnish with orange peel.

## ASTORIA MARTINI

1 ½ oz gin

½ oz dry vermouth

Dash of orange bitters

Green olive

Shake gin and vermouth with ice and strain into a chilled cocktail glass. Garnish with olive.

## BACARDI MARTINI

2 oz Bacardi white rum

½ oz dry vermouth

Orange peel

Shake rum and vermouth with ice and strain into a chilled cocktail glass. Garnish with orange peel.

## BANANA MARTINI

2 ½ oz vodka

¼ oz crème de banane

Splash of dry vermouth

Caramelized or candied banana

Shake vodka and crème de banane with ice and strain into a chilled cocktail glass. Garnish with banana.

## ATTA BOY MARTINI

2 oz gin

½ oz dry vermouth

2 dashes of grenadine syrup

Orange peel

Shake gin, vermouth, and grenadine with ice and strain into a chilled cocktail glass. Garnish with orange peel.

## BACARDI LIMÓN MARTINI

2 oz Bacardi Limón rum

¾ oz dry vermouth

Splash of cranberry juice

Lemon peel

Shake rum, vermouth, and juice with ice and strain into a chilled cocktail glass. Garnish with lemon peel.

## BANZAI MARTINI

2 ½ oz vodka

¼ oz ginjo sake

⅛ oz dry vermouth

Japanese pickled plum

Coat interior of a chilled cocktail glass with vermouth and discard remainder. Shake vodka and sake with ice and strain into the cocktail glass. Garnish with pickled plum.

*Atty Martini*

*Bacardi Sweet Martini*

Barbarella

## BARBARELLA

2 oz vodka

½ oz dry vermouth

2 gorgonzola-stuffed olives

Shake vodka and vermouth with ice and strain into a chilled cocktail glass. Garnish with olives.

## BEAUTY SPOT MARTINI

1 oz gin

½ oz dry vermouth

½ oz sweet vermouth

¼ oz orange juice

Dash of grenadine syrup

Pour the grenadine in the bottom of a chilled cocktail glass. Shake the gin, vermouths, and juice with ice and gently strain into the glass.

## BITTERSWEET MARTINI

1 ½ oz dry vermouth

1 ½ oz sweet vermouth

Dash of Angostura bitters

Dash of orange bitters

Orange peel

Shake vermouth and bitters with ice and strain into a chilled cocktail glass. Garnish with orange peel.

## BARON MARTINI

1 ½ oz gin

½ oz dry vermouth

¼ oz orange Curaçao

¼ oz sweet vermouth

Lemon peel

Shake gin, Curaçao, and vermouths with ice and strain into a chilled cocktail glass. Garnish with lemon peel.

## BIJOU COCKTAIL MARTINI

1 oz gin

1 oz Green Chartreuse

1 oz sweet vermouth

Dash of orange bitters

Maraschino cherry

Shake gin, Chartreuse, bitters, and vermouth with ice and strain into a chilled cocktail glass. Garnish with cherry.

## BLACK TIE MARTINI

1 ½ oz vodka

Splash of Scotch whisky

Splash of Campari

2 cocktail onions

1 black olive

Shake vodka, whisky, and Campari with ice and strain into a chilled cocktail glass. Garnish with onions and olive.

## BARRY MARTINI

1 ½ oz gin

¾ oz sweet vermouth

¼ oz white crème de menthe

Dash of Angostura bitters

Lemon twist

Shake gin, vermouth, and bitters with ice and strain into a chilled cocktail glass. Top with a float of crème de menthe and garnish with lemon twist.

## BIKINI MARTINI

1 oz citron vodka

1 oz coconut rum

1 oz pineapple juice

Pineapple wedge

Shake vodka, rum and pineapple juice with ice and strain into a chilled cocktail glass. Garnish with pineapple wedge.

## BLONDE MARTINI

2 ½ oz gin

¼ oz Lillet Blonde

Shake with ice and strain into a chilled cocktail glass.

## BLOODHOUND MARTINI

1 oz gin
½ oz Fragoli
½ oz dry vermouth
½ oz sweet vermouth
Strawberry

Shake gin, Fragoli, and vermouths with ice and strain into a chilled cocktail glass. Garnish with strawberry.

## BOMBAY MARTINI

3 oz Bombay Sapphire gin
½ oz dry vermouth
Blue cheese-stuffed olive

Shake gin and vermouth with ice and strain into a chilled cocktail glass. Garnish with olive.

## BREAKFAST MARTINI

2 ½ oz orange vodka
½ tsp orange marmalade
Orange peel

Shake vodka and marmalade with ice and strain into a chilled cocktail glass. Garnish with orange peel.

## BLOOD ORANGE MARTINI

1 ½ oz orange vodka
1 oz Campari
Splash of club soda

Stir in a mixing glass with ice and strain into a chilled cocktail glass.

## BONE DRY MARTINI

3 oz dry gin
Splash of dry vermouth
Olive

Rinse a chilled cocktail glass with the vermouth and discard the remainder. Pour in the gin and garnish with the olive.

## BRONX GOLDEN MARTINI

2 oz gin
⅛ oz dry vermouth
⅛ oz orange juice
⅛ oz sweet vermouth
1 egg yolk

Shake all ingredients thoroughly with ice and strain into a chilled cocktail glass.

## BLUE SAPPHIRE MARTINI

2 oz Bombay Sapphire gin
1 oz Blue Curaçao
½ oz dry vermouth
Maraschino cherry

Shake gin, Curaçao, and vermouth with ice and strain into a chilled cocktail glass. Garnish with cherry.

## BOSTON BULLET MARTINI

2 oz gin
½ oz dry vermouth
Almond-stuffed green olive

Shake gin and vermouth with ice and strain into a chilled cocktail glass. Garnish with olive.

## BRONX TERRACE MARTINI

1 ½ oz gin
½ oz dry vermouth
¾ oz fresh lime juice
Maraschino cherry

Shake gin, vermouth, and lime juice with ice and strain into a chilled cocktail glass. Garnish with cherry.

*Blue Sapphire Martini*

## BROWN COCKTAIL MARTINI

1 oz gin
1 oz gold rum
¾ oz dry vermouth

Shake ingredients with ice and strain into a chilled cocktail glass.

## CATALINA MARTINI

2 ½ oz vodka
½ oz dry vermouth
½ oz peach schnapps
Lemon peel soaked in
  Grand Marnier

Shake vodka, vermouth, and schnapps with ice and strain into a chilled cocktail glass. Garnish with lemon peel.

## CHOCOLATE MARTINI

1 ½ oz vodka
¼ oz Kahlúa
¾ oz Godiva liqueur

Shake ingredients with ice and strain into a chilled cocktail glass.

## CAJUN MARTINI

1 ½ oz Absolut Peppar
  vodka
¼ oz dry vermouth
Tomolive

Shake vodka and vermouth with ice and strain into a chilled cocktail glass. Garnish with tomolive.

## CHATTERLEY MARTINI

2 oz dry gin
½ oz dry vermouth
¼ oz orange Curaçao

Shake ingredients with ice and strain into a chilled cocktail glass.

## CHOCOLATE RASPBERRY MARTINI

1 ½ oz raspberry vodka
½ oz vanilla vodka
½ oz white crème de cacao

Shake ingredients with ice and strain into a chilled cocktail glass.

## CAPRICE MARTINI

1 ½ oz gin
½ oz Bénédictine
½ oz dry vermouth
Dash of orange bitters

Shake ingredients with ice and strain into a chilled cocktail glass.

## CHICAGO MARTINI

2 oz gin
½ oz Scotch whisky
Green olive

Shake gin and whisky with ice and strain into a chilled cocktail glass. Garnish with olive.

## CIGAR LOVER'S MARTINI

2 ½ oz Cognac
½ oz tawny port
Orange peel

Stir together Cognac and port with ice and strain into a chilled cocktail glass. Garnish with orange peel.

*Chocolate Martini*

## CITRON MARTINI

1 ½ oz citron vodka

½ oz Cointreau

Lemon slice

Shake vodka and Cointreau with ice and strain into a chilled cocktail glass. Garnish with lemon slice.

## CLUB COCKTAIL MARTINI

1 ½ oz gin

¾ oz sweet vermouth

¼ oz Yellow Chartreuse

Lemon peel

Shake gin, vermouth, and Chartreuse with ice and strain into a chilled cocktail glass. Garnish with lemon peel.

## CREOLE MARTINI

2 oz vodka

½ oz dry vermouth

1 small jalapeño pepper

Shake vodka and vermouth with ice and strain into a chilled cocktail glass. Garnish with jalapeño.

## CLARIDGE MARTINI

1 oz gin

1 oz dry vermouth

½ oz apricot brandy

½ oz Cointreau

Shake ingredients with ice and strain into a chilled cocktail glass.

## CONTINENTAL MARTINI

2 ½ oz vodka

⅛ oz dry vermouth

Lemon-stuffed olive

Shake vodka and vermouth with ice and strain into a chilled cocktail glass. Garnish with olive.

## CZARINA MARTINI

2 oz black cherry vodka

¼ oz apricot brandy

¼ oz dry vermouth

Dash of bitters

Shake ingredients with ice and strain into a chilled cocktail glass.

## CLASSIC DRY MARTINI

2 ½ oz gin

3 dashes of dry vermouth

Lemon peel or olive

Stir gin and vermouth with ice and strain into a chilled cocktail glass. Garnish with lemon peel or olive.

## COPENHAGEN MARTINI

1 oz aquavit

1 oz gin

½ oz dry vermouth

Olive

Shake aquavit, gin, and vermouth with ice and strain into a chilled cocktail glass. Garnish with olive.

## DAMN THE WEATHER MARTINI

1 ½ oz gin

½ oz sweet vermouth

¼ oz triple sec

½ oz orange juice

Shake ingredients with ice and strain into a chilled cocktail glass.

Citron Martini

Classic Dry Martini

## DEEP SEA MARTINI

1 ½ oz gin

1 oz dry vermouth

¼ oz Pernod

Dash of orange bitters

Lemon peel

Shake gin, vermouth, and Pernod with ice and strain into a chilled cocktail glass. Garnish with lemon peel.

## DEWEY MARTINI

1 ½ oz vodka

Splash of dry vermouth

Dash of orange bitters

Shake ingredients with ice and strain into a chilled cocktail glass.

## DIETRICH MARTINI

1 oz gin

1 oz vodka

½ oz dry vermouth

Olive

Shake gin, vodka, and vermouth with ice and strain into a chilled cocktail glass. Garnish with olive.

## DELMONICO MARTINI

1 oz gin

½ oz Cognac

½ oz dry vermouth

½ oz sweet vermouth

Dash of Angostura bitters

Orange peel

Shake gin, Cognac, vermouths, and bitters with ice and strain into a chilled cocktail glass. Garnish with orange peel.

## DIAMOND HEAD MARTINI

1 ½ oz gin

½ oz triple sec

¼ oz sweet vermouth

2 oz pineapple juice

Pineapple wedge

Shake gin, triple sec, vermouth, and juice with ice and strain into a chilled cocktail glass. Garnish with pineapple wedge.

## DIPLOMAT MARTINI

1 ½ oz dry vermouth

½ oz sweet vermouth

⅛ oz maraschino cherry juice

Dash of Angostura bitters

Lemon peel

Cherry

Shake vermouths, cherry juice, and bitters with ice and strain into a chilled cocktail glass. Garnish with lemon peel and cherry.

## DERNIER ROUND MARTINI

1 ½ oz gin

½ oz dry vermouth

¼ oz Cognac

¼ oz Cointreau

Dash of Angostura bitters

Shake ingredients with ice and strain into a chilled cocktail glass.

## DIANA MARTINI

1 ½ oz gin

¾ oz dry vermouth

¼ oz sweet vermouth

¼ oz Pernod

Lemon peel

Shake gin, vermouths, and Pernod with ice and strain into a chilled cocktail glass. Garnish with lemon peel.

## DIRTY MARTINI

3 oz gin

¼ oz olive brine

Dash of dry vermouth

2 olives

Stir together gin, olive brine, and vermouth with ice and strain into a chilled cocktail glass. Garnish with two olives.

*Dirty Martini*

## DIXIE MARTINI

2 oz gin

¼ oz dry vermouth

¼ oz Herbsaint

Shake ingredients with ice and strain into a chilled cocktail glass.

## EMERALD MARTINI

2 oz Bacardi Limón rum

Splash of dry vermouth

Splash of Midori melon liqueur

Shake ingredients with ice and strain into a chilled cocktail glass.

## FIBBER MCGEE MARTINI

2 oz gin

1 oz sweet vermouth

1 oz grapefruit juice

3 dashes of Angostura bitters

Shake ingredients with ice and strain into a chilled cocktail glass.

## DU BARRY COCKTAIL MARTINI

1 ½ oz gin

¾ oz dry vermouth

¼ oz Pernod

Dash of Angostura bitters

Orange slice

Shake gin, vermouth, Pernod, and bitters with ice and strain into a chilled cocktail glass. Garnish with orange slice.

## EXTRA DRY MARTINI

3 oz gin

Three drops of dry vermouth

Olive

Shake gin and vermouth with ice and strain into a chilled cocktail glass. Garnish with olive.

## FIFTH AVENUE MARTINI

1 ½ oz gin

½ oz dry vermouth

½ oz Fernet Branca

Shake ingredients with ice and strain into a chilled cocktail glass.

## ELEGANT MARTINI

1 ½ oz vodka

¼ oz Grand Marnier (plus a dash for a float)

Dash of dry vermouth

Stir ingredients with ice and strain into a chilled cocktail glass. Top with a float of Grand Marnier.

## FARE-THEE-WELL MARTINI

1 ½ oz gin

½ oz dry vermouth

¼ oz sweet vermouth

¼ oz orange Curaçao

Shake ingredients with ice and strain into a chilled cocktail glass.

## FIN DE SIÈCLE COCKTAIL MARTINI

1 ½ oz gin

¾ oz sweet vermouth

¼ oz Amer Picon

Dash of orange bitters

Shake ingredients with ice and strain into a chilled cocktail glass.

Fibber McGee Martini

## FLATIRON MARTINI

1 ½ oz orange vodka

1 ½ oz Lillet

Splash of triple sec

Rinse a chilled cocktail glass with triple sec and discard remainder. Stir vodka and Lillet with ice and strain into the glass.

## FRENCH MARTINI

2 oz vodka

½ oz Chambord

1 ½ oz pineapple juice

Shake ingredients with ice and strain into a chilled cocktail glass.

## GAZETTE MARTINI

1 ½ oz brandy

¾ oz sweet vermouth

⅛ oz lemon juice

⅛ oz simple syrup

Shake ingredients with ice and strain into a chilled cocktail glass.

## FLYING DUTCHMAN

1 ¾ oz gin

¼ oz dry vermouth

2 dashes of orange Curaçao

Shake ingredients with ice and strain into a chilled cocktail glass.

## FRUIT BURST MARTINI

1 oz vodka

½ oz dry vermouth

½ oz peach schnapps

½ oz blue Curaçao

Pineapple juice

Shake ingredients with ice and strain into a chilled cocktail glass.

## GENE TUNNEY MARTINI

1 ¾ oz gin

¾ oz dry vermouth

Dash of lemon juice

Dash of orange juice

Maraschino cherry

Shake gin, vermouth, and juices with ice and strain into a chilled cocktail glass. Garnish with cherry.

## FRANGELICO MARTINI

1 ¼ oz vodka

½ oz Tuaca liqueur

¼ oz Frangelico

Stir ingredients with ice and strain into a chilled cocktail glass.

## GARDEN MARTINI

2 oz vodka

3 drops of dry vermouth

Cherry tomato

Pickled asparagus spear

Shake vodka and vermouth with ice and strain into a chilled cocktail glass. Garnish with asparagus spear and cherry tomato.

## GIBSON MARTINI

1 ½ oz gin

½ oz dry vermouth

Pearl onion

Shake gin and vermouth with ice and strain into a chilled cocktail glass. Garnish with onion.

*Fruit Burst Martini*

## GILROY MARTINI

1 oz gin
1 oz cherry brandy
½ oz dry vermouth
½ oz lemon juice
4 dashes of orange bitters

Shake ingredients with ice and strain into a chilled cocktail glass.

## GODFATHER MARTINI

2 oz vodka
¼ oz amaretto
¼ oz Grand Marnier
¼ oz dry vermouth
Maraschino cherry
Orange peel

Shake vodka, amaretto, Grand Marnier, and vermouth with ice and strain into a chilled cocktail glass. Garnish with orange peel and cherry.

## GUARDS MARTINI

1 ¾ oz gin
¾ oz sweet vermouth
¼ oz orange Curaçao
Orange peel

Shake gin, vermouth, and Curaçao with ice and strain into a chilled cocktail glass. Garnish with orange peel.

## GINKA MARTINI

1 ½ oz gin
1 ½ oz vodka
½ oz dry vermouth
Lemon peel

Shake gin, vodka, and vermouth with ice and strain into a chilled cocktail glass. Garnish with lemon peel.

## GOLF MARTINI

1 ¾ oz gin
¾ oz dry vermouth
2 dashes of Angostura bitters

Shake ingredients with ice and strain into a chilled cocktail glass.

## H AND H MARTINI

1 ¾ oz gin
¾ oz Lillet
¼ oz orange Curaçao
Orange peel

Shake gin, Lillet, and curaçao with ice and strain into a chilled cocktail glass. Garnish with orange peel.

## GLOOM CHASER MARTINI

1 ½ oz gin
½ oz dry vermouth
2 dashes of grenadine syrup
2 dashes of Pernod

Shake ingredients with ice and strain into a chilled cocktail glass.

## GREAT SECRET MARTINI

1 ¾ oz gin
¾ oz Lillet
Dash of Angostura bitters
Orange peel

Shake gin, Lillet, and bitters with ice and strain into a chilled cocktail glass. Garnish with orange peel.

## HAKAM MARTINI

1 ¼ oz gin
1 ¼ oz sweet vermouth
¼ oz Cointreau
Dash of orange bitters
Maraschino cherry

Shake gin, vermouth, Cointreau, and bitters with ice and strain into a chilled cocktail glass. Garnish with cherry.

Gilroy Martini

Inspiration

## HARRY'S MARTINI

1 ¾ oz gin

¾ oz sweet vermouth

¼ oz Pernod

Mint sprigs

Stir gin, vermouth, and Pernod with ice and strain into a chilled cocktail glass. Garnish with mint.

## HONOLULU HURRICANE MARTINI

2 oz gin

¼ oz dry vermouth

¼ oz sweet vermouth

¼ oz pineapple juice

Shake ingredients in a mixing glass with ice and strain into a chilled cocktail glass.

## IN AND OUT MARTINI

2 oz gin

¼ oz dry vermouth

Lemon peel

Fill a mixing glass with ice and add vermouth. Swirl the ice and discard. Add the gin and shake well. Strain into a frosted cocktail glass and garnish with lemon peel.

## HASTY COCKTAIL

1 ¼ oz gin

¼ oz Green Chartreuse

Lemon peel

Shake gin and Chartreuse with ice and strain into a chilled cocktail glass. Garnish with lemon peel.

## IDEAL MARTINI

1 ½ oz gin

1 oz dry vermouth

⅛ oz fresh grapefruit juice

4 dashes of maraschino cherry juice

Maraschino cherry

Shake gin, vermouth, and juices with ice and strain into a chilled cocktail glass. Garnish with cherry.

## INCA MARTINI

1 oz gin

½ oz dry sherry

½ oz dry vermouth

½ oz sweet vermouth

Dash of Angostura bitters

Dash of orgeat syrup

Shake ingredients with ice and strain into a chilled cocktail glass.

## HONG KONG MARTINI

2 oz gin

1 oz dry vermouth

⅛ oz lime juice

¼ oz simple syrup

Dash of Angostura bitters

Shake ingredients in a mixing glass with ice and strain into a chilled cocktail glass.

## IMPERIAL COCKTAIL MARTINI

1 ½ oz gin

1 ½ oz dry vermouth

½ oz maraschino cherry juice

2 dashes of Angostura bitters

Maraschino cherry

Shake gin, vermouth, cherry juice, and bitters with ice and strain into a chilled cocktail glass. Garnish with cherry.

## INSPIRATION

1 oz gin

¼ oz Calvados

¼ oz dry vermouth

¼ oz Grand Marnier

Maraschino cherry

Shake gin, Calvados, vermouth, and Grand Marnier with ice and strain into a chilled cocktail glass. Garnish with cherry.

## INTERNATIONAL MARTINI

2 oz gin
¼ oz dry vermouth
¼ oz sweet vermouth
2 dashes of crème de cassis

Shake ingredients with ice and strain into a chilled cocktail glass.

## JUNGLE MARTINI

1 oz gin
¾ oz sweet vermouth
¾ oz pineapple juice
¾ oz medium sherry

Shake ingredients with ice and strain into a chilled cocktail glass.

## LAST ROUND MARTINI

1 oz gin
1 oz dry vermouth
¼ oz brandy
¼ oz Pernod

Shake ingredients with ice and strain into a chilled cocktail glass.

## JOURNALIST MARTINI

1 ½ oz gin
¼ oz dry vermouth
¼ oz sweet vermouth
Dash of Angostura bitters
Dash of lemon juice
Dash of orange curaçao

Shake ingredients with ice and strain into a chilled cocktail glass.

## JUPITER COCKTAIL MARTINI

1 ½ oz gin
¾ oz dry vermouth
⅛ oz orange juice
⅛ oz crème de violette

Shake ingredients with ice and strain into a chilled cocktail glass.

## LAST TANGO MARTINI

1 ½ oz gin
1 oz orange juice
½ oz Cointreau
½ oz dry vermouth
½ oz sweet vermouth

Shake ingredients with ice and strain into a chilled cocktail glass.

## JUDGETTE COCKTAIL MARTINI

1 oz gin
¾ oz dry vermouth
¾ oz peach brandy
⅛ oz lime juice
Maraschino cherry

Shake gin, vermouth, brandy, and lime juice with ice and strain into a chilled cocktail glass. Garnish with cherry.

## KNICKERBOCKER MARTINI

1 ½ oz gin
1 ½ oz dry vermouth
2 dashes of orange bitters
Lemon peel

Shake gin, vermouth, and bitters with ice and strain into a chilled cocktail glass. Garnish with lemon peel.

## LEAP YEAR MARTINI

1 ¼ oz gin
½ oz orange-flavored gin
½ oz sweet vermouth
¼ oz lemon juice
¼ oz triple sec

Shake ingredients with ice and strain into a chilled cocktail glass.

Journalist Martini

## LILLET COCKTAIL MARTINI

1 ½ oz Lillet

1 oz gin

Lemon twist

Shake Lillet and gin with ice and strain into a chilled cocktail glass. Garnish with lemon twist.

## MAGNIFICENT SEVEN

2 ¼ oz vodka

Splash of cranberry juice

Splash of dry vermouth

Splash of sweet and sour

Splash of triple sec

Sugar

Lemon peel

Shake vodka, juice, vermouth, sweet and sour, and triple sec with ice and strain into a chilled cocktail glass rimmed with sugar. Garnish with lemon peel.

## MAXIM MARTINI

2 oz gin

1 oz sweet vermouth

2 dashes of white crème de cacao

Shake ingredients with ice and strain into a chilled cocktail glass.

## LOUIS MARTINI

1 ½ oz gin

½ oz dry vermouth

¼ oz Cointreau

¼ oz Grand Marnier

Lemon peel

Shake gin, vermouth, Cointreau, and Grand Marnier with ice and strain into a chilled cocktail glass. Garnish with lemon peel.

## MALIBU MARTINI

2 oz gin

½ oz Malibu rum

⅛ oz dry vermouth

Lemon peel

Shake gin, rum, and vermouth with ice and strain into a chilled cocktail glass. Garnish with lemon peel.

## MENTHE MARTINI

1 oz gin

1 oz dry vermouth

¼ oz white crème de menthe

Mint sprig

Shake gin, vermouth, and crème de menthe with ice and strain into a chilled cocktail glass. Garnish with mint sprig.

## LOYAL MARTINI

2 oz vodka

3 drops of high-quality balsamic vinegar

Shake ingredients with ice and strain into a chilled cocktail glass.

## MARTINEZ COCKTAIL

1 oz Old Tom gin

4 oz sweet vermouth

1 dash of Angostura bitters

2 dashes of maraschino liqueur

Shake ingredients with ice and strain into a chilled cocktail glass.

## MERVYN-TINI

2 ½ oz Stolichnaya Hot vodka

¼ oz dry vermouth

Caper berry

Shake gin and vermouth with ice and strain into a chilled cocktail glass. Garnish with caper berry.

*Magnificent Seven*

*Martinez Cocktail*

### MANDARIN MARTINI

1 ½ oz vodka

1 oz gin

Dash of Cointreau

¼ oz orange juice

Mandarin orange section

Shake vodka, gin, Cointreau, and juice with ice and strain into a chilled cocktail glass. Garnish with orange section.

### MOULIN ROUGE MARTINI

1 ½ oz sloe gin

¾ oz sweet vermouth

3 dashes of Angostura bitters

Shake ingredients with ice and strain into a chilled cocktail glass.

### NICK AND NORA MARTINI

1 ½ oz gin

½ oz dry vermouth

Olive

Shake gin and vermouth with ice and strain into a chilled cocktail glass. Garnish with olive.

### MODDER COCKTAIL MARTINI

1 ½ oz gin

½ oz dry vermouth

½ oz Dubonnet

Lemon peel

Shake gin, vermouth, and Dubonnet with ice and strain into a chilled cocktail glass. Garnish with lemon peel.

### NEGRONI MARTINI

1 ½ oz gin

1 ½ oz sweet vermouth

¾ oz Campari

Lemon peel

Shake gin, vermouth, and Campari with ice and strain into a chilled cocktail glass. Garnish with lemon peel.

### NUMBER 3 MARTINI

1 ¾ oz gin

½ oz dry vermouth

¼ oz anisette

Dash of Angostura bitters

Shake ingredients with ice and strain into a chilled cocktail glass.

### MOTHER'S DAY MARTINI

3 oz vodka

Dash of dry vermouth

Dash of rose water

3 fresh rose petals

Stir vodka, vermouth, and rose water gently with ice and strain into a chilled cocktail glass. Garnish with rose petals.

### NEW YORKER MARTINI

1 ½ oz dry vermouth

½ oz gin

½ oz dry sherry

Dash of Cointreau

Shake ingredients with ice and strain into a chilled cocktail glass.

### OLD ESTONIAN MARTINI

1 ¼ oz gin

1 ¼ oz Lillet

2 dashes of crème de noyaux

2 dashes of orange bitters

Orange peel

Shake gin, Lillet, crème de noyaux, and bitters with ice and strain into a chilled cocktail glass. Garnish with orange peel.

*Nick And Nora Martini*

*New Yorker Martini*

## OPERA MARTINI

1 ½ oz gin

½ oz Dubonnet

⅛ oz maraschino cherry
  juice

Shake ingredients with ice and
strain into a chilled cocktail glass.

## PALMETTO MARTINI

1 ½ oz rum

1 oz sweet vermouth

2 dashes of bitters

Lemon peel

Shake rum, vermouth, and bitters
with ice and strain into a chilled
cocktail glass. Garnish with
lemon peel.

## PEPPER MARTINI

2 oz pepper vodka

½ oz dry vermouth

Jalapeño-stuffed olive

Shake vodka and vermouth with
ice and strain into a chilled
cocktail glass. Garnish with olive.

## ORANGE MARTINI

2 oz vodka

¼ oz Grand Marnier

3 dried cherries

Orange peel

Rub the inside of a chilled cocktail
glass with the orange peel. Shake
vodka and Grand Marnier with ice
and strain into the cocktail glass.
Garnish with cherries.

## PARISIAN MARTINI

1 oz gin

1 oz crème de cassis

1 oz dry vermouth

Shake ingredients with ice and
strain into a chilled cocktail glass.

## PERFECT MARTINI

1 ¾ oz gin

¼ oz dry vermouth

¼ oz sweet vermouth

Lemon peel

Shake gin and vermouths with ice
and strain into a chilled cocktail
glass. Garnish with lemon peel.

## PAISLEY MARTINI

2 oz gin

½ oz dry vermouth

½ oz Highland Scotch
  whisky

Lemon peel

Shake gin, vermouth, and whisky
with ice and strain into a chilled
cocktail glass. Garnish with
lemon peel.

## PARK AVENUE MARTINI

1 ½ oz gin

1 oz pineapple juice

½ oz sweet vermouth

2-3 drops of Curaçao

Shake ingredients with ice and
strain into a chilled cocktail glass.

## PERFECT ROYAL MARTINI

¾ oz gin

¾ oz dry vermouth

¾ oz sweet vermouth

¼ oz Pernod

Green cherry

Shake gin, vermouth, and Pernod
with ice and strain into a chilled
cocktail glass. Garnish with cherry.

211

*Perfect Martini*

Pink Martini

## PERNOD MARTINI

2 oz gin

½ oz dry vermouth

2 dashes of Pernod

Shake ingredients with ice and strain into a chilled cocktail glass.

## POET'S DREAM MARTINI

1 oz gin

¾ oz Bénédictine

¾ oz dry vermouth

Lemon peel

Shake gin, Bénédictine, and vermouth with ice and strain into a chilled cocktail glass. Garnish with lemon peel.

## PSYCHEDELIC MARTINI

2 oz gin

¼ oz dry vermouth

¼ oz sweet vermouth

½ oz orange juice

½ oz pineapple juice

Dash of anisette

Shake ingredients with ice and strain into a chilled cocktail glass.

## PINEAU MARTINI

1 oz gin

2 oz Pineau des Charentes

Shake ingredients with ice and strain into a chilled cocktail glass.

## POLO MARTINI CLUB

1 oz gin

½ oz dry vermouth

½ oz sweet vermouth

¼ oz lime juice

Shake ingredients with ice and strain into a chilled cocktail glass.

## PURITAN MARTINI

1 ¾ oz gin

½ oz dry vermouth

¼ oz Yellow Chartreuse

Dash of orange bitters

Shake ingredients with ice and strain into a chilled cocktail glass.

## PINK MARTINI

1 ½ oz vodka

½ oz cranberry juice

Dash of dry vermouth

Lime wedge

Shake vodka, juice, and vermouth with ice and strain into a chilled cocktail glass. Garnish with lime wedge.

## POMEGRANATE MARTINI

2 oz vodka

½ oz Cointreau

2 oz pomegranate juice

Splash of lime juice

Shake ingredients with ice and strain into a chilled cocktail glass.

## QUEEN ELIZABETH MARTINI

1 ½ oz gin

Dash of dry vermouth

Splash of Bénédictine

Lemon peel

Shake gin, vermouth, and Bénédictine with ice and strain into a chilled cocktail glass. Garnish with lemon peel.

## R.A.C.

2 oz gin

¼ oz vermouth

Dash of grenadine syrup

Dash of orange bitters

Maraschino cherry

Orange peel

Shake gin, vermouth, syrup, and bitters with ice and strain into a chilled cocktail glass. Garnish with cherry and orange peel.

## RED GIN MARTINI

2 oz gin

½ oz sloe gin

⅛ oz dry vermouth

Orange peel

Shake gin and vermouth with ice and strain into a chilled cocktail glass. Garnish with orange peel.

## ROLLS ROYCE MARTINI

2 oz gin

1 oz sweet vermouth

½ oz Bénédictine

½ oz dry vermouth

Shake ingredients with ice and strain into a chilled cocktail glass.

## RASPBERRY VODKA MARTINI

1 ½ oz raspberry vodka

Splash of Chambord

Lime peel

Shake vodka and Chambord with ice and strain into a chilled cocktail glass. Garnish with lime peel.

## RED RIM MARTINI

1 oz vodka

1 ½ oz raspberry-white grape juice

Sweet vermouth to rim

Red sugar to rim

Blackberry

Rim a chilled cocktail glass with sweet vermouth and red sugar. Shake vodka and juice with ice and strain into the cocktail glass. Garnish with a blackberry.

## ROMA MARTINI

1 ½ oz gin

½ oz dry vermouth

½ oz sweet vermouth

3 strawberries

Shake ingredients, including strawberries, and pour into a chilled cocktail glass.

## RED APPLE MARTINI

¾ oz gin

¾ oz sweet vermouth

½ oz apple brandy

½ oz grenadine syrup

Shake ingredients with ice and strain into a chilled cocktail glass.

## RICHMOND MARTINI

1 ¾ oz gin

¾ oz Lillet

Lemon peel

Shake vodka and Lillet with ice and strain into a chilled cocktail glass. Garnish with lemon peel.

## ROSA MARTINI

1 ½ oz gin

¼ oz cherry brandy

¼ oz dry vermouth

Lemon twist

Shake gin, cherry brandy, and vermouth with ice and strain into a chilled cocktail glass. Garnish with lemon twist.

*Raspberry Vodka Martini*

Saratoga Martini

## ROSALIND RUSSELL MARTINI

1 ½ oz gin

Dash of aquavit

Lemon peel

Shake gin and aquavit with ice and strain into a chilled cocktail glass. Garnish with lemon peel.

## ROSY MARTINI

2 oz citrus vodka

½ oz Cointreau

½ oz Dubonnet

Shake ingredients with ice and strain into a chilled cocktail glass.

## SALT-AND-PEPPER MARTINI

2 ½ oz pepper vodka

Coarse salt

Lemon wedge

Cocktail onion

Rim a chilled cocktail glass with salt, using the lemon wedge. Pour in the vodka and garnish with onion.

## ROSE DU BOY

1 ½ oz gin

½ oz dry vermouth

¼ oz cherry brandy

¼ oz kirschwasser

Shake ingredients with ice and strain into a chilled cocktail glass.

## RUM MARTINI

2 oz light rum

¼ oz dry vermouth

Lemon peel

Shake rum and vermouth with ice and strain into a chilled cocktail glass. Garnish with lemon peel.

## SAN FRANCISCO COCKTAIL MARTINI

¾ oz dry vermouth

¾ oz sweet vermouth

¾ oz sloe gin

Dash of Angostura bitters

Dash of orange bitters

Maraschino cherry

Shake vermouth, gin, and bitters with ice and strain into a chilled cocktail glass. Garnish with cherry.

## ROSE MARIE MARTINI

1 ¼ oz gin

½ oz dry vermouth

¼ oz Armagnac

¼ oz Campari

¼ oz cherry brandy

Shake ingredients with ice and strain into a chilled cocktail glass.

## SAKETINI

2 ½ oz gin

¼ oz sake

¼ oz orange Curaçao

Cucumber slice

Stir vodka, sake, and Curaçao with ice and strain into a chilled cocktail glass. Garnish with cucumber.

## SARATOGA MARTINI

1 ½ oz vodka

2 dashes of Angostura bitters

2 dashes of grenadine syrup

Splash of soda water

Pineapple wedge

Shake vodka, syrup, and bitters with ice and strain into a chilled cocktail glass. Top with soda and garnish with pineapple wedge.

## SAVOY HOTEL SPECIAL MARTINI

1 ½ oz gin

½ oz dry vermouth

2 dashes of grenadine syrup

Dash of Pernod

Lemon peel

Shake gin, vermouth, syrup, and Pernod with ice and strain into a chilled cocktail glass. Garnish with lemon peel.

## SELF-STARTER MARTINI

1 ½ oz gin

¾ oz Lillet

¼ oz apricot brandy

2 dashes of Pernod

Shake ingredients with ice and strain into a chilled cocktail glass.

## SMILER MARTINI

1 ¼ oz gin

½ oz dry vermouth

½ oz sweet vermouth

¼ oz orange juice

Dash of Angostura bitters

Shake ingredients with ice and strain into a chilled cocktail glass.

## SAVOY MARTINI

1 ¾ oz gin

½ oz dry vermouth

¼ oz Dubonnet

Orange peel

Shake gin, vermouth, and Dubonnet with ice and strain into a chilled cocktail glass. Garnish with orange peel.

## SILVER BULLET MARTINI

1 ½ oz gin

Dash of dry vermouth

⅛ oz blended Scotch whisky

Shake gin and vermouth with ice and strain into a chilled cocktail glass. Top with a float of whisky.

## SMOKY MARTINI

2 ½ oz gin

Splash of Islay Scotch whisky

Lemon peel

Stir gin and whisky with ice and strain into a chilled cocktail glass. Garnish with lemon peel.

## SCHNOZZLE MARTINI

¾ oz gin

¾ oz dry vermouth

½ oz medium sherry

¼ oz orange Curaçao

¼ oz Pernod

Shake ingredients with ice and strain into a chilled cocktail glass.

## SLOE VERMOUTH MARTINI

1 oz dry vermouth

1 oz sloe gin

⅓ oz lemon juice

Shake ingredients with ice and strain into a chilled cocktail glass.

## S'MORE MARTINI

2 oz vodka

½ oz chocolate liqueur

⅛ oz sweet vermouth

Shake ingredients with ice and strain into a chilled cocktail glass.

Smoky Martini

## SOVIET MARTINI

2 oz vodka

½ oz Manzanilla sherry

Splash of dry vermouth

Lemon peel

Stir vodka, sherry, and vermouth with ice and strain into a chilled cocktail glass. Garnish with lemon peel.

## STAR COCKTAIL MARTINI

1 ½ oz apple brandy

1 ½ oz sweet vermouth

2 dashes of Angostura bitters

Lemon peel

Stir brandy, vermouth, and bitters with ice and strain into a chilled cocktail glass. Garnish with lemon peel.

## SUSHI MARTINI

2 ½ oz gin

¼ oz dry vermouth

Pinch of pickled ginger

Tobiko-stuffed olive

Shake gin and vermouth with ice and strain into a chilled cocktail glass. Garnish with ginger and olive.

## SPHINX MARTINI

2 oz gin

¾ oz dry vermouth

¼ oz sweet vermouth

Lemon wedge

Shake gin and vermouth with ice and strain into a chilled cocktail glass. Garnish with lemon wedge.

## SUPERMODEL MARTINI

2 oz Bacardi Limón rum

½ oz Blue Curaçao

½ oz melon liqueur

Splash of dry vermouth

Shake ingredients with ice and strain into a chilled cocktail glass.

## TANGO COCKTAIL MARTINI

1 oz gin

½ oz sweet vermouth

½ oz dry vermouth

⅛ oz triple sec

½ oz orange juice

Shake ingredients with ice and strain into a chilled cocktail glass.

## SAKE MARTINI

2 oz vodka

¼ oz gin

¼ oz sake

Cucumber slice

Shake vodka, gin, and sake with ice and strain into a chilled cocktail glass. Garnish with cucumber.

## SUPPER MARTINI

2 oz gin

Dash of Drambuie liqueur

Dash of sweet vermouth

Maraschino cherry

Shake gin, Drambuie, and vermouth with ice and strain into a chilled cocktail glass. Garnish with cherry.

## TATOU'S TATOUNI

2 ½ oz vodka

¼ oz dry vermouth

⅛ oz cucumber juice

Cucumber slice

Shake vodka, vermouth, and cucumber juice with ice and strain into a chilled cocktail glass. Garnish with cucumber slice.

Stake Martini

Tatou's Tatouni

Van Martini

## TONIGHT OR NEVER MARTINI

1 oz gin
1 oz dry vermouth
½ oz Cognac

Shake ingredients with ice and strain into a chilled cocktail glass.

## UPSIDE-DOWN MARTINI

2 ½ oz dry vermouth
1 oz gin

Shake ingredients with ice and strain into a chilled cocktail glass.

## VERMOUTH TRIPLE SEC MARTINI

1 oz gin
1 oz dry vermouth
½ oz triple sec
2 dashes of orange bitters
Lemon peel

Shake gin, vermouth, triple sec, and bitters with ice and strain into a chilled cocktail glass. Garnish with lemon peel.

## TRILBY MARTINI

1 ¼ oz gin
1 oz sweet vermouth
2 dashes of orange bitters
¼ oz Chambord

Stir the gin, vermouth, and bitters with ice and strain into a chilled cocktail glass. Top with a float of Chambord.

## VAN MARTINI

1 ¾ oz gin
½ oz dry vermouth
¼ oz Grand Marnier

Shake ingredients with ice and strain into a chilled cocktail glass.

## VESPER

1 ½ oz gin
½ oz vodka
¼ oz Lillet Blonde
Orange peel

Shake gin, vodka, and Lillet with ice and strain into a chilled cocktail glass. Garnish with orange peel.

## TUXEDO MARTINI

1 ¼ oz gin
1 ¼ oz dry vermouth
¼ oz maraschino cherry juice
Dash of Pernod
2 dashes of orange bitters
Lemon peel

Shake gin, vermouth, cherry juice, Pernod, and bitters with ice and strain into a chilled cocktail glass. Garnish with lemon peel.

## VENDOME MARTINI

1 oz Beefeater gin
1 oz Dubonnet
½ oz dry vermouth
Orange peel

Shake gin, Dubonnet, and vermouth with ice and strain into a chilled cocktail glass. Garnish with orange peel.

## VICTOR MARTINI

1 ½ oz dry vermouth
½ oz gin
½ oz brandy

Shake ingredients with ice and strain into a chilled cocktail glass.

## VODKA GIBSON MARTINI

2 ½ oz vodka

⅛ oz dry vermouth

Cocktail onion

Shake vodka and vermouth with ice and strain into a chilled cocktail glass. Garnish with onion.

## WHITE ANGEL MARTINI

1 ¼ oz gin

1 ¼ oz vodka

Olive

Shake the gin and vodka with ice and strain into a chilled cocktail glass. Garnish with an olive.

## WINSTON MARTINI

1 oz gin

1 oz spiced rum

Dash of Frangelico

Small dash of lime juice

Lemon peel

Rinse a chilled cocktail glass with the Frangelico. Shake the gin, rum, and lime juice with ice and strain into the cocktail glass. Garnish with lemon peel.

## VODKA MARTINI

1 ½ oz vodka

½ oz dry vermouth

Olive

Shake vodka and vermouth with ice and strain into a chilled cocktail glass. Garnish with olive.

## WEMBLEY MARTINI

1 ½ oz gin

¾ oz dry vermouth

¼ oz apple brandy

Dash of apricot brandy

Shake ingredients with ice and strain into a chilled cocktail glass.

## XANTHIA MARTINI

1 ½ oz gin

1 oz Cointreau

1 oz dry vermouth

Stir ingredients with ice and strain into a chilled cocktail glass.

## WALTER MARTINI

2 oz gin

½ oz dry sherry

½ oz dry vermouth

2 drops of lemon juice

Shake ingredients with ice and strain into a chilled cocktail glass.

## WILD ROSE MARTINI

1 ½ oz gin

½ oz dry vermouth

½ oz sweet vermouth

Dash of Angostura bitters

Dash of orange bitters

Shake ingredients with ice and strain into a chilled cocktail glass.

## YALE COCKTAIL MARTINI

1 ½ oz gin

½ oz dry vermouth

⅛ oz blue Curaçao

Dash of bitters

Stir ingredients with ice and strain into a chilled cocktail glass.

*Yale Cocktail Martini*

Yellow Rattler

## YALE MARTINI

1 ½ oz gin

½ oz dry vermouth

¼ oz maraschino cherry juice

2 dashes of orange bitters

Table or powdered sugar

Shake gin, vermouth, cherry juice, and bitters with ice and strain into a chilled cocktail glass. Add sugar to taste.

## YELLOW DAISY MARTINI

1 ½ oz gin

½ oz dry vermouth

¼ oz Grand Marnier

¼ oz Pernod

Maraschino cherry

Shake gin, vermouth, Grand Marnier, and Pernod with ice and strain into a chilled cocktail glass. Garnish with cherry.

## YELLOW RATTLER

2 oz gin

1 oz dry vermouth

Dash of orange bitters

2 cocktail onions

Shake gin, vermouth, and bitters with ice and strain into a chilled cocktail glass. Garnish with onions.

## YOLANDA MARTINI

¾ oz gin

¾ oz brandy

½ oz sweet vermouth

¼ oz grenadine

¼ oz Pernod

Stir ingredients with ice and strain into a chilled cocktail glass.

## ZANZIBAR MARTINI

2 ½ oz dry vermouth

1 oz gin

½ oz lemon juice

⅛ oz simple syrup

3 dashes of Angostura bitters

Lemon peel

Stir vermouth, gin, juice, syrup, and bitters with ice and strain into a chilled cocktail glass. Garnish with lemon peel.

*Yolanda Martini*

# G R E A T
## COCKTAIL BARS
### O F  T H E  W O R L D

Almost every major city contains at least one first-class cocktail bar, but some are exceptional.

### NEW YORK

More than any other city, New York is the home of the cocktail, and some of its legendary hotel bars—Bemelman's in the Carlyle, the Blue Bar at the Algonquin—retain their glamour to this day. Other classic bars include the Old Town Bar in the Flatiron district and the well worn P. J. Clarke's on 3rd Avenue.

### LONDON AND PARIS

While the Savoy has long been considered the pinnacle of London's cocktail culture, other bars have emerged that equal or surpass the Savoy, such as the Connaught Bar at the Connaught Hotel in Mayfair. And no cocktail safari in London would be complete without a visit to Dukes Bar, at the Dukes Hotel in St. James, where Ian Fleming threw back many a martini. In Paris, there's Harry's New York Bar in Les Halles/Rivoli—birthplace of the Sidecar and the haunt of writers, artists, and sophisticates for decades. But La Palette in St.-Germain, the one-time haunt of Picasso, has its own rich history and old-school feel, without so much hauteur.

White Lady

Sidecar

## ABBEY COCKTAIL

1 ½ oz gin
¾ oz Lillet Blonde
1 oz orange juice
Dash of bitters
Orange peel

Shake gin, Lillet, juice, and bitters with ice and strain into a chilled cocktail glass. Garnish with orange peel.

## ALEXANDER

1 oz gin
1 oz dark crème de cacao
2 oz heavy cream
Grated nutmeg

Shake gin, crème de cacao, and heavy cream with ice and strain into a chilled cocktail glass. Dust with nutmeg.

## AMERICAN BEAUTY

1 oz brandy
1 oz dry vermouth
1 oz orange juice
2 dashes of grenadine syrup
½ oz port
Rose petal

Shake brandy, vermouth, orange juice, and grenadine with ice and strain into a chilled cocktail glass. Top with a float of port and garnish with rose petal.

## ABSOLUTELY BANANAS

1 ½ oz vodka
½ oz banana liqueur
1 ½ oz pineapple juice

Shake ingredients with ice and strain into a chilled cocktail glass.

## ALGONQUIN

2 oz light rum
½ oz blackberry brandy
½ oz Bénédictine
½ oz lime juice
Cherry

Stir rum, brandy, Bénédictine, and lime juice with ice and strain into a chilled cocktail glass. Garnish with cherry.

## APPLEJACK COCKTAIL

2 oz applejack or Calvados
¾ oz orange Curaçao
½ oz lime juice
2 dashes of orange bitters
Apple slice
Orange peel

Shake applejack, curaçao, lime juice, and bitters with ice and strain into a chilled cocktail glass. Garnish with apple slice and orange peel.

## ALASKA COCKTAIL

1 ½ oz gin
¾ oz Yellow Chartreuse
2 dashes of orange bitters

Stir ingredients with ice and strain into a chilled cocktail glass.

## AMARETTO ALEXANDER

1 oz amaretto
1 oz dark crème de cacao
1 oz heavy cream

Shake ingredients with ice and strain into a chilled cocktail glass.

## APPLE MANHATTAN

2 oz bourbon
¾ oz apple schnapps
¼ oz triple sec
½ oz sweet vermouth

Shake ingredients with ice and strain into a chilled cocktail glass.

*Alexander*

## AQUEDUCT

1 ½ oz vodka
½ oz triple sec
½ oz apricot brandy
½ oz lime juice

Shake ingredients with ice and strain into a chilled cocktail glass.

## BALLET RUSSE

2 oz vodka
1 oz crème de cassis
¼ oz lime juice

Shake ingredients with ice and strain into a chilled cocktail glass.

## BEACHCOMBER

2 oz light rum
¾ oz Cointreau
¾ oz lime juice
¼ oz maraschino liqueur
Ice

Combine all ingredients in a blender and blend to desired consistency.

## AVIATION COCKTAIL

2 oz gin
1 oz maraschino liqueur
¼ oz lemon juice
Lemon peel

Shake gin, liqueur, and juice with ice and strain into a chilled cocktail glass. Garnish with lemon peel.

## BALM COCKTAIL

2 oz medium sherry
¾ oz orange juice
½ oz Cointreau
2 dashes of Angostura bitters
2 orange slices
Orange peel

Shake all ingredients except orange peel with ice and strain into a chilled cocktail glass. Garnish with orange peel.

## BEE'S KISS

1 ½ oz light rum
1 oz heavy cream
¾ oz honey syrup (equal parts honey and warm water, mixed and then chilled)

Shake ingredients with ice and strain into a chilled cocktail glass.

## BACARDI COCKTAIL

1 ½ oz Bacardi Light
1 oz lemon juice
1 oz simple syrup
3 dashes of grenadine syrup

Shake ingredients with ice and strain into a chilled cocktail glass.

## BANSHEE

1 oz crème de banane
1 oz white crème de cacao
2 oz heavy cream

Shake ingredients with ice and strain into a chilled cocktail glass.

## BEE'S KNEES

2 oz gin
¾ oz honey syrup (equal parts honey and warm water, mixed and then chilled)
½ oz lemon juice

Shake ingredients with ice and strain into a chilled cocktail glass.

*Aviation Cocktail*

Blue Monday

## BETWEEN THE SHEETS

1 ½ oz brandy

½ oz Bénédictine

½ oz Cointreau

¾ oz lemon juice

Orange peel

Shake brandy, Bénédictine, Cointreau, and juice with ice and strain into a chilled cocktail glass. Garnish with orange peel.

## BLUE MONDAY

1 ½ oz vodka

½ oz Cointreau

¼ oz Blue Curaçao

Orange peel

Shake all ingredients but orange peel with ice and strain into a chilled cocktail glass. Garnish with orange peel.

## BOLO COCKTAIL

2 oz rum

½ oz lime juice

1 oz orange juice

2 dashes of Angostura bitters

Shake ingredients with ice and strain into a chilled cocktail glass.

## BLACKTHORN

2 ½ oz Irish whiskey

½ oz dry vermouth

2 dashes of Angostura bitters

2 dashes of Pernod

Lemon peel

Shake whiskey, vermouth, Pernod, and bitters with ice and strain into a chilled cocktail glass. Garnish with lemon peel.

## BLUE TRAIN

1 ½ oz gin

½ oz Cointreau

¼ oz lemon juice

Dash of Blue Curaçao

Orange peel

Shake all ingredients but orange peel with ice and strain into a chilled cocktail glass. Garnish with orange peel.

## BOSTON SIDECAR

1 oz light rum

½ oz brandy

½ oz triple sec

½ oz lime juice

Shake ingredients with ice and strain into a chilled cocktail glass.

## BLOOD AND SAND

¾ oz Scotch whisky

¾ oz Cherry Heering

¾ oz sweet vermouth

1 oz orange juice

Orange peel

Shake all ingredients but the orange peel with ice and strain into a chilled cocktail glass. Garnish with orange peel.

## BOBBY BURNS

2 oz Scotch whisky

1 oz sweet vermouth

¼ oz Bénédictine

Shortbread cookie

Stir whisky, vermouth, and Bénédictine with ice and strain into a chilled cocktail glass. Garnish with cookie.

## BOULEVARD

2 oz rye whiskey

½ oz Grand Marnier

½ oz dry vermouth

Orange peel

Stir whiskey, Grand Marnier, and vermouth with ice and strain into a chilled cocktail glass. Garnish with orange peel.

## BRANDY ALEXANDER

1 oz brandy

1 oz dark crème de cacao

2 oz heavy cream

Grated nutmeg

Shake brandy, crème de cacao, and heavy cream with ice and strain into a chilled cocktail glass. Dust with nutmeg.

## BRASSY BLONDE

2 oz lemon vodka

2 oz pineapple juice

¼ oz Cointreau

Shake ingredients with ice and strain into a chilled cocktail glass.

## BROWN DERBY COCKTAIL

2 oz bourbon

1 oz grapefruit juice

½ oz honey syrup (equal parts honey and warm water, mixed and then chilled)

Shake ingredients with ice and strain into a chilled cocktail glass.

## BRANDY COCKTAIL

2 oz brandy

½ oz orange Curaçao

2 dashes of Angostura bitters

2 dashes of Peychaud's bitters

Lemon peel

Shake all ingredients but lemon peel with ice and strain into a chilled cocktail glass. Garnish with lemon peel.

## BRONX COCKTAIL

1 ½ oz gin

¼ oz sweet vermouth

¼ oz dry vermouth

1 ½ oz orange juice

Orange peel

Shake all ingredients but orange peel with ice and strain into a chilled cocktail glass. Garnish with orange peel.

## BULL'S BLOOD

¾ oz rum

¾ oz orange Curaçao

¾ oz Spanish brandy

1 ½ oz orange juice

Orange peel

Shake all ingredients but orange peel with ice and strain into a chilled cocktail glass. Garnish with orange peel.

## BRANDY CRUSTA

1 ½ oz brandy

¼ oz maraschino liqueur

¼ oz Cointreau

¼ oz lemon juice

Lemon peel

Sugar

Using the lemon peel, sugar the rim of a chilled cocktail glass. Shake brandy, liqueurs, and lemon juice with ice and strain into the glass. Garnish with lemon peel.

## BROOKLYN COCKTAIL

2 oz Canadian whisky

1 oz dry vermouth

Dash of maraschino liqueur

Dash of Amer Picon

Lemon peel

Shake all ingredients but lemon peel with ice and strain into a chilled cocktail glass. Garnish with lemon peel.

## CABLE CAR

1 ½ oz Captain Morgan spiced rum

¾ oz orange Curaçao

1 oz lemon juice

½ oz simple syrup

Cinnamon sugar

Orange peel

Using orange peel, rim a chilled cocktail glass with cinnamon sugar. Shake rum, curaçao, lemon juice, and syrup with ice and strain into the cocktail glass. Garnish with orange peel.

*Brandy Alexander*

*Brandy Crusta*

## CAMPARI VICEROY

2 oz Campari
½ oz Southern Comfort
½ oz amaretto
Splash of orange juice
Splash of pineapple juice

Shake ingredients with ice and strain into a chilled cocktail glass.

## CLOVER CLUB

1 ½ oz gin
¾ oz simple syrup
¾ oz raspberry syrup
¾ oz lemon juice
Half an egg white

Shake ingredients with ice and strain into a chilled cocktail glass.

## COFFEE ALEXANDER

1 oz brandy
1 oz Kahlúa
1 oz heavy cream

Shake ingredients with ice and strain into a chilled cocktail glass.

## CHARLIE CHAPLIN

1 oz apricot brandy
1 oz sloe gin
1 oz lime juice
Lime peel

Shake brandy, gin, and juice with ice and strain into a chilled cocktail glass. Garnish with lime peel.

## CLUB COCKTAIL

2 oz brandy
½ oz maraschino liqueur
½ oz pineapple juice
2 dashes of Peychaud's bitters
1 strawberry
Lemon peel

Shake brandy, maraschino liqueur, juice, and bitters with ice and strain into a chilled cocktail glass. Garnish with strawberry and lemon peel.

## COOPERSTOWN

2 oz gin
½ oz sweet vermouth
½ oz dry vermouth
2 sprigs mint

In a mixing glass, muddle one sprig of mint with the vermouths. Add gin and ice, stir, and strain into a chilled martini glass. Garnish with remaining mint sprig.

## CHERRY BLOSSOM

1 ½ oz brandy
½ oz Cherry Heering
½ oz orange Curaçao
½ oz lemon juice
5 sour cherries, pitted

In a mixing glass, muddle the cherries with the lemon juice, Cherry Heering, and Curaçao. Add the brandy, shake with ice, and strain into a chilled cocktail glass.

## COCTEL ALGERIA

¾ oz pisco
¾ oz Cointreau
¾ oz apricot brandy
1 oz orange juice
Orange peel

Shake all ingredients except orange peel with ice and strain into a chilled cocktail glass. Garnish with orange peel.

## CORPSE REVIVER

1 oz gin
½ oz Cointreau
½ oz Lillet Blonde
¾ oz lemon juice
Dash of absinthe

Shake ingredients with ice and strain into a chilled cocktail glass.

*Campari Viceroy*

Cosmopolitan

Daiquiri

## COSMOPOLITAN

1 ½ oz citron vodka

½ oz Cointreau

¼ oz lime juice

1 oz cranberry juice

Orange peel

Shake all ingredients but orange peel with ice and strain into a chilled cocktail glass. Garnish with orange peel.

## DERBY COCKTAIL

2 ½ oz gin

¼ oz peach liqueur

½ peach, quartered

Mint sprig, with a few leaves set aside

In a mixing glass, muddle the peach, mint leaves and peach liqueur. Add the gin and shake with ice. Strain into a chilled cocktail glass and garnish with mint sprig.

## D.O.M. COCKTAIL

2 oz gin

1 oz orange juice

½ oz Bénédictine

Orange peel

Shake all ingredients but orange peel with ice and strain into a chilled cocktail glass. Garnish with orange peel.

## DAIQUIRI

1 ½ oz light rum

1 oz simple syrup

¾ oz lime juice

Shake ingredients with ice and strain into a chilled cocktail glass.

## DESHLER COCKTAIL

1 ½ oz Dubonnet

1 ½ oz rye

¼ oz Cointreau

Dash of Angostura bitters

Orange peel

Shake all ingredients except orange peel with ice and strain into a chilled cocktail glass. Garnish with orange peel.

## DOROTHY

2 oz silver rum

½ oz orange juice

½ oz pineapple juice

¼ oz Apry apricot liqueur

Orange peel

Shake all ingredients but orange peel with ice and strain into a chilled cocktail glass. Garnish with orange peel.

## DEBONAIRE COCKTAIL

2 ½ oz Highland single-malt Scotch whisky

¾ oz Canton Ginger liqueuer

Stir ingredients with ice and strain into a chilled cocktail glass.

## DEVIL'S TORCH

1 ½ oz vodka

1 ½ oz dry vermouth

3 dashes of grenadine syrup

Lemon peel

Shake vodka, vermouth, and grenadine with ice and strain into a chilled cocktail glass. Garnish with lemon peel.

## DUBONNET COCKTAIL

1 ½ oz Dubonnet

1 ½ oz gin

Lemon peel

Stir Dubonnet and gin with ice and strain into a chilled cocktail glass. Garnish with lemon peel.

## ELK'S OWN

1 oz Canadian whisky

1 oz port

½ oz lemon juice

¼ oz simple syrup

1 small egg white

Shake ingredients with ice and strain into a chilled cocktail glass.

## ESPRESSO COCKTAIL

¾ oz vodka

¾ oz Kahlúa

1 oz espresso, chilled

Brown sugar

Rim a chilled cocktail glass with brown sugar. Shake the other ingredients with ice and strain into the cocktail glass.

## FLAMINGO

1 ½ oz white rum

1 ½ oz pineapple juice

¼ oz lime juice

¼ oz grenadine syrup

Shake ingredients with ice and strain into a chilled cocktail glass.

## EL PRESIDENTE

1 ½ oz light rum

1 ½ oz dry vermouth

½ oz orange Curaçao

¼ oz grenadine syrup

Orange peel

Shake all ingredients but orange peel with ice and strain into a chilled cocktail glass. Garnish with orange peel.

## FERNET BRANCA COCKTAIL

2 oz gin

½ oz Fernet Branca

¾ oz sweet vermouth

Lemon peel

Stir gin, Fernet Branca, and vermouth with ice and strain into a cocktail glass. Garnish with lemon peel.

## FRENCH FLAMINGO

1 oz Absolut Kurant vodka

1 oz Cointreau

¾ oz lime juice

¾ oz pomegranate juice

Shake ingredients with ice and strain into a chilled cocktail glass.

## EMBASSY COCKTAIL

¾ oz brandy

¾ oz Cointreau

¾ oz Appleton Estate rum

½ oz lime juice

Dash of Angostura bitters

Lime piece

Shake all ingredients but lime piece with ice and strain into a chilled cocktail glass. Garnish with lime piece.

## FLAME OF LOVE

2 ½ oz vodka

½ oz fino sherry

Several orange peels

Coat the inside of a chilled cocktail glass with the sherry, discarding remainder. Gently flame several orange peels by lightly squeezing each peel by its edges and gently snapping your wrist with one hand over a lit match in the other hand a couple of inches above the drink, so that the oils in the peel ignite briefly as they fall into the glass. Stir the vodka in a mixing glass with ice and strain into the cocktail glass. Garnish with one of the orange peels.

## GERSHWIN

2 oz gin

¾ oz lemon juice

½ oz ginger syrup

½ oz simple syrup

Dash of rose water

Candied ginger slice

Shake gin, juice, and syrups with ice and strain into a chilled cocktail glass. Spritz with rose water and garnish with candied ginger.

*Embassy Cocktail*

*Espresso Cocktail*

## GIMLET

2 ½ oz gin

½ oz preserved lime juice

Lime wedge

Shake the gin and juice with ice and strain into a chilled cocktail glass. Garnish with lime wedge.

## GOLDEN CADILLAC

1 oz Galliano

1 oz white crème de cacao

2 oz heavy cream

Cinnamon

Shake Galliano, crème de cacao, and cream with ice and strain into a chilled cocktail glass. Dust with cinnamon.

## HAPPY HONEY COCKTAIL

2 oz brandy

1 oz grapefruit juice

½ oz honey syrup (equal parts honey and warm water, mixed and then chilled)

Shake ingredients with ice and strain into a chilled cocktail glass.

## GIN ALEXANDER

2 oz gin

1 oz white crème de cacao

½ oz heavy cream

Grated nutmeg

Shake gin, crème de cacao, and cream with ice and strain into a chilled cocktail glass. Dust with nutmeg.

## GOLDEN DAWN

½ oz gin

¾ oz apricot brandy

¾ oz orange juice

Dash of grenadine syrup

2 dashes of bitters

Orange slice

Cherry

Shake gin, brandy, juice, bitters, and syrup with ice and strain into a chilled cocktail glass. Garnish with orange slice and cherry.

## HARRY'S COCKTAIL

2 oz gin

1 oz sweet vermouth

2 dashes of Absente

3 sprigs of mint

Stuffed olive

In a mixing glass, muddle two of the mint sprigs with the vermouth and Absente. Add the gin and shake with ice. Strain into a chilled cocktail glass and garnish with remaining mint sprig and olive.

## GIN AND IT

1 ½ oz gin

1 ½ oz sweet vermouth

Dash of Angostura bitters

Orange peel

Shake gin, vermouth, and bitters with ice and strain into a chilled cocktail glass. Garnish with orange peel.

## GRASSHOPPER

1 oz green crème de menthe

1 oz white crème de cacao

2 oz heavy cream

Shake ingredients with ice and strain into a chilled cocktail glass.

## HEMINGWAY DAIQUIRI

1 ½ oz white rum

¾ oz lime juice

½ oz grapefruit juice

Dash of maraschino liqueur

Shake ingredients with ice and strain into a chilled cocktail glass.

*Gimlet*

*Gin And It*

*Grasshopper*

Katana

## HI HO COCKTAIL

2 oz gin

1 oz white port

4 dashes of orange bitters

Lemon peel

Shake gin, port, and bitters with ice and strain into a chilled cocktail glass. Garnish with lemon peel.

## HONOLULU COCKTAIL

2 oz gin

½ oz pineapple juice

½ oz orange juice

¼ oz lemon juice

¼ oz simple syrup

Dash of Angostura bitters

Lemon peel

Sugar the rim of a chilled cocktail glass. Shake the gin, juices, syrup, and bitters with ice and strain into the cocktail glass. Garnish with lemon peel.

## JAPANESE COCKTAIL

2 oz Cognac

½ oz orgeat syrup

½ oz lime juice

Dash of Angostura bitters

Lime peel

Shake all ingredients but lime peel with ice and strain into a chilled cocktail glass. Garnish with lime peel.

## HILGERT COCKTAIL

1 oz dry vermouth

¾ oz gin

⅛ oz maraschino liqueur

¼ oz grapefruit juice

Dash of Angostura bitters

Shake ingredients with ice and strain into a chilled cocktail glass.

## INTERNATIONAL STINGER

2 oz Metaxa

¾ oz Galliano

Shake ingredients with ice and strain into a chilled cocktail glass.

## KATANA

1 ½ oz vodka

½ oz sake

¾ oz lime juice

¾ oz simple syrup

3 cucumber slices

In a mixing glass, muddle two cucumber slices with the lime juice and syrup. Add vodka and sake and shake with ice. Strain into a chilled cocktail glass and garnish with remaining cucumber slice.

## HONEYMOON COCKTAIL

2 oz apple brandy

½ oz Bénédictine

½ oz orange Curaçao

½ oz lemon juice

Lemon peel

Shake all ingredients but lemon peel with ice and strain into a chilled cocktail glass. Garnish with lemon peel.

## ISLAND ROSE

¾ oz tequila

¾ oz Kahlúa

½ oz Chambord

1 ½ oz heavy cream

Rose petal

Shake all ingredients but the rose petal with ice and strain into a chilled cocktail glass. Garnish with rose petal.

## KNICKERBOCKER

2 oz rum

½ oz orange Curaçao

½ oz raspberry syrup

¾ oz lemon juice

1 lemon wedge

Shake all ingredients, including squeezed lemon wedge, with ice and strain into a chilled cocktail glass.

## LEMON DROP

2 oz citrus vodka

½ oz Cointreau

¼ oz lemon juice

Lemon wheel

Sugar the rim of a chilled cocktail glass. Shake the vodka, Cointreau, and lemon juice with ice and strain into the cocktail glass. Float the lemon wheel on top.

## MADISON AVENUE COCKTAIL

1 ½ oz white rum

¾ oz Cointreau

½ oz lime juice

Dash of orange bitters

Mint sprig, with three leaves removed

Lime peel

Shake the rum, Cointreau, lime juice, mint leaves, and bitters with ice and strain into a chilled cocktail glass. Garnish with mint sprig and lime peel.

## MARK TWAIN COCKTAIL

1 ½ oz Islay Scotch whisky

¾ oz lemon juice

1 oz simple syrup

2 dashes of Angostura bitters

Lemon peel

Shake all ingredients but lemon peel with ice and strain into a chilled cocktail glass. Garnish with lemon peel.

## LEO SPECIAL

1 ½ oz gin

1 oz Cointreau

¾ oz lime juice

Dash of Pernod

Dash of green crème de menthe

Shake ingredients with ice and strain into a chilled cocktail glass.

## MANHATTAN

2 oz rye or bourbon whiskey

1 oz sweet vermouth

2 dashes of Angostura bitters

Cherry

Stir the whiskey, vermouth, and bitters with ice in a mixing glass and strain into a chilled cocktail glass. Garnish with cherry.

## MARY PICKFORD

2 oz white rum

1 ½ oz pineapple juice

⅛ oz grenadine syrup

¼ oz maraschino liqueur

Shake ingredients with ice and strain into a chilled cocktail glass.

## LIMEY COCKTAIL

1 oz white rum

1 oz lime vodka

½ oz triple sec

½ oz lime juice

Lime peel

Shake all ingredients but lime peel with ice and strain into a chilled cocktail glass. Garnish with lime peel.

## MARAGATO

1 oz silver rum

½ oz sweet vermouth

½ oz dry vermouth

1 oz orange juice

½ oz lime juice

Dash of maraschino liqueur

Orange peel

Shake all ingredients but orange peel with ice and strain into a chilled cocktail glass. Garnish with orange peel.

## MERRY WIDOW

2 oz gin

½ oz dry vermouth

Dash of Absente

Dash of Angostura bitters

Dash of Bénédictine

Lemon peel

Swirl the Absente in a chilled cocktail glass and discard remainder. In a mixing glass, stir the gin, vermouth, Bénédictine, and bitters and strain into the cocktail glass. Garnish with lemon peel.

Lemon Drop

Manhattan

## METROPOLITAN

1 ½ oz Absolut Kurant
   vodka
1 ½ oz cranberry juice
½ oz preserved lime juice
⅛ oz fresh lime juice
Lime wedge

Shake all ingredients but lime
wedge with ice and strain into
a chilled cocktail glass. Garnish
with lime wedge.

## NATIONAL COCKTAIL

1 ½ oz white rum
1 ½ oz pineapple juice
½ oz lemon juice
Dash of apricot brandy

Shake ingredients with ice and
strain into a chilled cocktail glass.

## PARADISE COCKTAIL

2 oz gin
¾ oz Marie Brizard Apry
¾ oz orange juice
2 dashes of orange bitters
Orange peel

Shake gin, Apry, juice, and bitters
with ice and strain into a chilled
cocktail glass. Garnish with
orange peel.

## MILLION-DOLLAR COCKTAIL

1 ½ oz gin
½ oz sweet vermouth
½ oz pineapple juice
½ small egg white
2 dashes of grenadine
   syrup

Shake ingredients with ice and
strain into a chilled cocktail glass.

## NUTTY ANGEL

1 oz vodka
1 oz Frangelico
1 oz Bailey's Irish Cream
½ oz dark crème de cacao
Grated nutmeg

Shake ingredients (except
nutmeg) with ice and strain into
a chilled cocktail glass. Dust with
nutmeg.

## PARIS

1 oz gin
1 oz dry vermouth
1 oz crème de cassis
Lemon peel

Shake gin, vermouth, and crème
de cassis with ice and strain into
a chilled cocktail glass. Garnish
with lemon peel.

## MONKEY GLAND

2 oz gin
1 ½ oz orange juice
⅛ oz grenadine syrup
Splash of Ricard
Flamed orange peel

Shake all ingredients but the
orange peel with ice and strain
into a chilled cocktail glass.
Garnish with orange peel.

## ORANGE BLOSSOM

2 oz gin
1 oz orange juice
½ oz simple syrup
Orange peel

Shake gin, juice, and syrup with
ice and strain into a chilled
cocktail glass. Garnish with
orange peel.

## PARISIAN BLONDE

1 oz rum
1 oz orange Curaçao
1 oz heavy cream
Vanilla extract

Shake rum, Curaçao, and cream
with ice and strain into a chilled
cocktail glass. Sprinkle with a
couple of drops of vanilla extract
if desired.

*Orange Blossom*

*Pink Lady*

## PARIS WHEN IT SIZZLES

2 oz aged rum

½ oz lime juice

¾ oz elderflower liqueur

Dash of Angostura bitters

Lime wedge

Shake rum, lime juice, liqueur, and bitters with ice and strain into a chilled cocktail glass. Garnish with lime wedge.

## PINEAPPLE COCKTAIL

1 ½ oz light rum

¾ oz pineapple juice

⅛ oz lemon juice

Shake ingredients with ice and strain into a chilled cocktail glass.

## PINK SQUIRREL

¾ oz crème de noyaux

¾ oz white crème de cacao

1 ½ oz heavy cream

Shake ingredients with ice and strain into a chilled cocktail glass.

## PEACH MELISSA

1 ½ oz dark rum

½ oz simple syrup

1 oz orange juice

¼ oz lemon juice

1 oz peach puree

Peach slice

Shake all ingredients but peach slice with ice and strain into a chilled cocktail glass. Garnish with peach slice.

## PINK GIN

2 oz gin

3 dashes of Angostura bitters

Lemon peel

Shake gin and bitters with ice and strain into a chilled cocktail glass. Garnish with lemon peel.

## PREAKNESS COCKTAIL

2 oz rye whiskey

¾ oz Carpano Antica vermouth

¼ oz Bénédictine

2 dashes of Angostura bitters

Stir ingredients with ice and strain into a chilled cocktail glass.

## PEGU COCKTAIL

2 oz gin

¾ oz Curaçao

2 dashes of Angostura bitters

4 lime wedges

Lime peel

In the bottom of a mixing glass, muddle the lime pieces, Curaçao, and bitters. Add the gin and shake with ice. Strain into a chilled cocktail glass and garnish with lime peel.

## PINK LADY

1 ½ oz gin

¼ oz grenadine

¾ oz simple syrup

1 oz heavy cream

Shake ingredients with ice and strain into a chilled cocktail glass.

## PRESIDENTE

1 ½ oz white rum

¾ oz orange Curaçao

¾ oz dry vermouth

Dash of grenadine

Shake ingredients with ice and strain into a chilled cocktail glass.

## RED LION

1 oz Grand Marnier

1 oz dry gin

½ oz orange juice

½ oz lemon juice

Orange peel

Shake Grand Marnier, gin, and juices with ice and strain into a chilled cocktail glass. Garnish with orange peel.

## ROYAL COCKTAIL

1 ½ oz gin

¾ oz dry vermouth

¾ oz Cherry Heering

Lemon peel

Stir gin, vermouth, and Cherry Heering with ice and strain into a chilled cocktail glass. Garnish with lemon peel.

## SATAN'S WHISKERS

1 oz gin

½ oz sweet vermouth

½ oz dry vermouth

½ oz Grand Marnier

1 oz orange juice

Dash of Angostura bitters

Orange peel

Shake all ingredients but orange peel with ice and strain into a chilled cocktail glass. Garnish with orange peel.

## RED MANHATTAN

2 ½ oz vodka

¾ oz St. Raphael

2 dashes of Angostura bitters

Shake ingredients with ice and strain into a chilled cocktail glass.

## ROYAL HAWAIIAN

1 ½ oz gin

½ oz lemon juice

1 oz pineapple juice

¼ oz orgeat syrup

Shake ingredients with ice and strain into a chilled cocktail glass.

## SCARLETT O'HARA

2 oz Southern Comfort

½ oz lime juice

1 oz cranberry juice

Shake ingredients with ice and strain into a chilled cocktail glass.

## ROB ROY

2 ½ oz Scotch whisky

1 oz sweet vermouth

Dash of Angostura bitters

Lemon peel

Stir whisky, vermouth, and bitters with ice and strain into a chilled cocktail glass. Garnish with lemon peel.

## ROYAL ROMANCE

1 ½ oz gin

½ oz Grand Marnier

1 oz passion fruit nectar

2 dashes of grenadine syrup

Orange peel

Shake all ingredients but orange peel with ice and strain into a chilled cocktail glass. Garnish with orange peel.

## SHERRY COCKTAIL

2 ½ oz fino sherry

½ oz Absente

½ oz maraschino liqueur

Orange peel

Shake all ingredients but orange peel with ice and strain into a chilled cocktail glass. Garnish with orange peel.

*Rob Roy*

Toasted Almond

## SOUTH COAST COCKTAIL (SERVES TWO)

2 ½ oz Scotch whisky
½ oz Curaçao
½ oz lemon juice
¼ oz simple syrup
2 ½ oz club soda
2 orange peels

Stir all ingredients but the orange peels in a mixing glass and strain evenly into two chilled cocktail glasses. Garnish each with an orange peel.

## SUNTORY COCKTAIL

1 ½ oz citrus vodka
1 oz Midori melon liqueur
1 oz grapefruit juice

Shake ingredients with ice and strain into a chilled cocktail glass.

## TULIP COCKTAIL

¾ oz apple brandy
¾ oz sweet vermouth
½ oz apricot brandy
½ oz lemon juice

Shake ingredients with ice and strain into a chilled cocktail glass.

## STILETTO

1 oz amaretto
½ oz banana liqueur
1 oz pineapple juice
Orange peel

Shake all ingredients but orange peel with ice and strain into a chilled cocktail glass. Garnish with orange peel.

## TOASTED ALMOND

¾ oz amaretto
¾ oz Kahlúa
2 oz heavy cream

Shake ingredients with ice and strain into a chilled cocktail glass.

## TWENTIETH CENTURY

2 oz gin
¼ oz white crème de cacao
½ oz Lillet Blonde
¼ oz lemon juice

Shake ingredients with ice and strain into a chilled cocktail glass.

## STORK CLUB COCKTAIL

1 ½ oz gin
½ oz triple sec
¼ oz lime juice
1 oz orange juice
Dash of Angostura bitters
Orange peel

Shake all ingredients but orange peel with ice and strain into a chilled cocktail glass. Garnish with orange peel.

## TROPICAL COCKTAIL

2 oz white rum
¾ oz orange Curaçao
½ oz lime juice

Shake ingredients with ice and strain into a chilled cocktail glass.

## VALENCIA COCKTAIL

1 ½ oz apricot brandy
½ oz orange juice
2 dashes of orange bitters

Shake ingredients with ice and strain into a chilled cocktail glass.

## VANDERBILT COCKTAIL

1 ½ oz brandy

¾ oz cherry brandy

¼ oz simple syrup

2 dashes of Angostura bitters

Shake ingredients with ice and strain into a chilled cocktail glass.

## WALDORF

2 oz bourbon

¾ oz sweet vermouth

2 dashes of Angostura bitters

Splash of Ricard

Swirl the Ricard in a mixing glass and discard remainder. Add bourbon, vermouth, and bitters with ice and stir. Strain into a chilled cocktail glass.

## WOODWARD COCKTAIL

1 ½ oz Scotch whisky

½ oz dry vermouth

½ oz grapefruit juice

Shake ingredients with ice and strain into a chilled cocktail glass.

## VELVET HAMMER

¾ oz triple sec

¾ oz white crème de cacao

2 oz heavy cream

Grated nutmeg

Shake triple sec, crème de cacao, and cream with ice and strain into a chilled cocktail glass. Dust with nutmeg.

## WALTERS

1 ½ oz Scotch whisky

½ oz orange juice

½ oz lemon juice

Shake ingredients with ice and strain into a chilled cocktail glass.

## YELLOW BIRD

2 oz rum

½ oz triple sec

½ oz Galliano

¾ oz lime juice

Lime peel

Shake rum, triple sec, Galliano, and lime juice with ice and strain into a chilled cocktail glass. Garnish with lime peel.

## VENDÔME

1 oz Dubonnet

1 oz gin

1 oz dry vermouth

Lemon peel

Stir Dubonnet, gin, and vermouth with ice and strain into a chilled cocktail glass. Garnish with lemon peel.

## WHITE LADY

1 ½ oz gin

1 oz lemon juice

1 oz Cointreau

Shake ingredients with ice and strain into a chilled cocktail glass.

*White Lady*

# SHOTS &
## SHOOTERS

SHOTS AND SHOOTERS ARE THE MOST RECREATIONAL
OF COCKTAILS. DESPITE THEIR POPULAR IMAGE, MOST
OF THEM ARE ACTUALLY RATHER LOW IN ALCOHOL; THE
DANGER OF SHOTS LIES IN THE TEMPTATION TO DRINK
TOO MANY, TOO QUICKLY. GIVEN HOW DELICIOUS MANY
OF THEM ARE, THAT CAN BE ALL TOO EASY TO DO.

## AFFAIR

1 oz strawberry schnapps
1 oz cranberry juice
1 oz orange juice

Stir ingredients with ice and strain into a chilled cordial glass.

## ANGEL'S DELIGHT

¼ oz grenadine
¼ oz triple sec
¼ oz sloe gin
¼ oz light cream

Layer the ingredients in a cordial glass in the order listed, from the bottom up.

## ANGEL'S WING

½ oz white crème de cacao
½ oz brandy
½ oz light cream

Layer the ingredients in a cordial glass in the order listed, from the bottom up.

## AFTER FIVE

½ oz Kahlúa
½ oz Bailey's Irish Cream
½ oz peppermint schnapps

Layer the ingredients in a cordial glass in the order listed, from the bottom up.

## ANGEL'S KISS

¼ oz white crème de cacao
¼ oz sloe gin
¼ oz brandy
¼ oz light cream

Layer the ingredients in a cordial glass in the order listed, from the bottom up.

## B-52

½ oz Kahlúa
½ oz Bailey's Irish Cream
½ oz Mandarine Napoléon

Layer the ingredients in a cordial glass in the order listed, from the bottom up.

## ALABAMA SLAMMER

1 oz amaretto
1 oz Tennessee whiskey
½ oz sloe gin
Splash of lemon juice

Stir amaretto, whiskey, and gin with ice and strain into a chilled shot glass. Add lemon juice.

## ANGEL'S TIP

¼ oz white crème de cacao
¼ oz light cream
Maraschino cherry

In a cordial glass, float the cream over the crème de cacao and garnish with cherry.

## BANANA BOMBER

1 oz banana schnapps
¾ oz triple sec
Splash of grenadine

Shake ingredients with ice and strain into a chilled shot glass.

B-52

## BANANA SLIP

1 ½ oz crème de banane
1 ½ oz Bailey's Irish Cream

In a cordial glass, float the Bailey's on the crème de banane.

## BLUE MARLIN

1 oz light rum
½ oz Blue Curaçao
1 oz lime juice

Stir ingredients with ice and strain into a chilled shot glass.

## BONZAI PIPELINE

½ oz vodka
1 oz tropical fruit schnapps

Stir ingredients with ice and strain into a chilled shot glass.

## BETWEEN THE SHEETS

1 oz lemon juice
½ oz brandy
½ oz triple sec
½ oz light rum

Shake ingredients with ice and strain into a chilled shot glass.

## BLOW JOB

¼ oz Bailey's Irish Cream
½ oz amaretto
Whipped cream

Combine the Bailey's and amaretto in a shot glass and top with whipped cream.

## BUTTERY NIPPLE

1 oz Buttershots liqueur
½ oz Bailey's Irish Cream

Float the Bailey's on the Buttershots in a chilled shot glass.

## BLOODY CAESAR SHOOTER

1 littleneck clam
1 oz vodka
2 drops of Worcestershire sauce
1 ½ oz tomato juice
2 drops of Tabasco sauce
Dash of horseradish sauce
Pinch of celery salt
Lime wedge

Put the clam in the bottom of a shot glass. Shake all other ingredients but the celery salt and lime with ice and strain into the shot glass. Sprinkle with celery salt and garnish with lime wedge.

## BOILERMAKER

1 ½ oz whiskey
12 oz lager

Drop a shot glass of the whiskey into a pint glass of the lager.

## BUZZARD'S BREATH

½ oz amaretto
½ oz peppermint schnapps
½ oz coffee liqueur

Stir ingredients with ice and strain into a chilled shot glass.

*Between The Sheets*

*Cement Mixer*

## CAPRI

¾ oz white crème de cacao

¾ oz crème de banane

¾ oz light cream

Shake ingredients with ice and strain into a chilled cordial glass.

## CHARLIE CHAPLIN

1 oz sloe gin

1 oz apricot brandy

1 oz lemon juice

Shake ingredients with ice and strain into a chilled cordial glass.

## COSMOS

1 ½ oz vodka

½ oz lime juice

Shake ingredients with ice and strain into a chilled shot glass.

## CARAMEL APPLE

1 oz apple schnapps

1 oz butterscotch schnapps

Shake ingredients with ice and strain into a chilled shot glass.

## CHOCOLATE CAKE

¾ oz citrus vodka

¾ oz Frangelico

Lemon coated in sugar

Shake vodka and Frangelico with ice and strain into a cordial glass. Serve with sugar-coated lemon, which should be sucked as a chaser.

## FIFTH AVENUE

½ oz dark crème de cacao

½ oz apricot brandy

½ oz light cream

Layer the ingredients in a cordial glass in the order listed, from the bottom up.

## CEMENT MIXER

1 ½ oz Bailey's Irish Cream

½ oz lime juice

In a shot glass, float the lime juice on the Bailey's.

## CORDLESS SCREWDRIVER

1 ¾ oz vodka

Orange wedge

Sugar

Shake vodka with ice and strain into a shot glass. Dip the orange wedge in sugar. The orange wedge should be sucked as a chaser.

## FLYING GRASSHOPPER

¾ oz green crème de menthe

¾ oz white crème de cacao

¾ oz vodka

Stir ingredients with ice and strain into a chilled cordial glass.

## FOURTH OF JULY TOOTER

1 oz grenadine syrup

1 oz vodka

1 oz Blue Curaçao

Layer the ingredients in a cordial glass in the order listed, from the bottom up.

## GREEN DEMON

½ oz vodka

½ oz rum

½ oz Midori melon liqueur

½ oz lemonade

Shake ingredients with ice and strain into a chilled shot glass.

## IRISH CHARLIE

1 oz Bailey's Irish Cream

1 oz white crème de menthe

Stir with ice and strain into a chilled cordial glass.

## FOXY LADY

1 oz amaretto

½ oz crème de cacao

1 oz heavy cream

Shake ingredients with ice and strain into a chilled cordial glass.

## INTERNATIONAL INCIDENT

¼ oz vodka

¼ oz Kahlúa

¼ oz amaretto

¼ oz Frangelico

½ oz Irish Cream liqueur

Shake ingredients with ice and strain into a chilled shot glass.

## IRISH FLAG

1 oz green crème de menthe

1 oz Bailey's Irish Cream

1 oz Mandarine Napoléon

Layer the ingredients in a cordial glass in the order listed, from the bottom up.

## GALACTIC ALE

¾ oz vodka

¾ oz Blue Curaçao

½ oz lime juice

¼ oz black raspberry liqueur

Shake ingredients with ice and strain into a chilled shot glass.

## IRISH BOMB

¾ pint Guinness Stout

½ shot Bailey's Irish Cream

½ shot Irish whiskey

Layer the whiskey on the Bailey's in a shot glass, and drop the shot glass in the pint glass of Guinness.

## JÄGER BOMB

1 ½ oz Jägermeister

½ can Red Bull energy drink

Fill a shot glass with the Jägermeister. Drop the shot glass into a highball glass filled with Red Bull.

*Galactic Ale*

*Irish Flag*

*Jello Shot*

*Kamikaze*

## JELLO SHOT

3 oz Jell-O or other gelatin, in the flavor of choice
1 cup boiling water
½ cup vodka, chilled
½ cup cold water

Dissolve the gelatin in the boiling water. Add the cold vodka and water, and pour into plastic shot cups. Refrigerate for at least two hours.

## KAMIKAZE

½ oz vodka
½ oz triple sec
½ oz lime juice

Shake ingredients with ice and strain into a chilled shot glass.

## LIQUID COCAINE

⅓ oz Jägermeister
⅓ oz cinnamon schnapps
⅓ oz peppermint schnapps

Shake ingredients with ice and strain into a chilled shot glass.

## JELLY BEAN

½ oz grenadine
½ oz anisette
½ oz Southern Comfort

Layer the ingredients in a shot glass in the order listed, from the bottom up.

## KOOL AID

½ oz Midori melon liqueur
½ oz amaretto
½ oz cranberry juice

Stir ingredients with ice and strain into a chilled shot glass.

## MELON BALL

1 oz Midori melon liqueur
1 oz vodka
1 oz pineapple juice

Shake ingredients with ice and strain into a chilled cordial glass.

## JOHNNY ON THE BEACH

¾ oz vodka
½ oz Midori melon liqueur
½ oz black raspberry liqueur
¼ oz pineapple juice
¼ oz orange juice
¼ oz grapefruit juice
¼ oz cranberry juice

Shake ingredients with ice and strain into a chilled shot glass.

## LEMON DROP

1 ½ oz vodka, chilled
Lemon wedge
Sugar

Fill a shot glass with the chilled vodka and serve with sugared lemon wedge. The lemon wedge is to be sucked on as a chaser.

## MIND ERASER

1 oz vodka
1 oz Kahlúa
Club soda
Lime wedge

Fill an old-fashioned glass with ice, add vodka and Kahlúa, and top with soda. Serve with a straw, which is to be used for drinking, rather than stirring.

## MOCHA MINT

¾ oz coffee brandy

¾ oz white crème de cacao

¾ oz white crème de menthe

Shake ingredients with ice and strain into a chilled cordial glass.

## NUTTY PROFESSOR

½ oz Mandarine Napoléon

½ oz Frangelico

½ oz Bailey's Irish Cream

Combine liqueurs in a shot glass.

## OYSTER SHOOTER

1 raw oyster

1 tsp spicy cocktail sauce

1 tsp horseradish

1 tsp lemon juice

Pinch of black pepper

1 shot of pepper vodka

Drop the oyster in a shot glass. Top with the other ingredients and stir.

## MONKEY SHINE SHOOTER

½ oz bourbon liqueur

½ oz crème de banane

½ oz Bailey's Irish Cream

Shake ingredients with ice and strain into a chilled shot glass.

## OH MY GOSH

1 oz amaretto

1 oz peach schnapps

Stir ingredients with ice and strain into a chilled shot glass.

## PARISIAN BLONDE SHOOTER

¾ oz light rum

¾ oz triple sec

¾ oz gold rum

Shake ingredients with ice and strain into a chilled cordial glass.

## NUTTY IRISHMAN

¾ oz Bailey's Irish Cream

¾ oz Frangelico

Combine liqueurs in a shot glass.

## ORGASM

⅓ oz amaretto

⅓ oz Kahlúa

⅓ oz Bailey's Irish Cream

Shake ingredients with ice and strain into a chilled shot glass.

## PEACH BUNNY

¾ oz peach brandy

¾ oz white crème de cacao

¾ oz light cream

Shake ingredients with ice and strain into a chilled cordial glass.

*Orgasm*

## PEACH TART

1 oz peach schnapps

½ oz lime juice

Stir ingredients with ice and strain into a chilled shot glass.

## PICKLEBACK

1 ½ oz Jameson's Irish whiskey

1 ½ oz pickle juice

Pour a shot each of Jameson's and pickle juice. The Jameson's is to be drunk first and held in the mouth, then the pickle juice added.

## PRAIRIE FIRE

1 oz tequila

3 drops of hot sauce of choice

Combine ingredients in a shot glass.

## PEANUT BUTTER AND JELLY

¾ oz Frangelico

¾ oz Chambord

Shake ingredients with ice and strain into a chilled shot glass.

## PIGSKIN SHOT

1 oz vodka

1 oz Midori melon liqueur

½ oz simple syrup

¼ oz lemon juice

Shake ingredients with ice and strain into a chilled shot glass.

## PURPLE HOOTER

1 ½ oz citrus vodka

½ oz triple sec

¼ oz black raspberry liqueur

Shake ingredients with ice and strain into a chilled shot glass.

## PEPPERMINT PATTY

1 oz white crème de cacao

1 oz white crème de menthe

Shake ingredients with ice and strain into a chilled cordial glass.

## PINEAPPLE UPSIDE-DOWN CAKE

½ oz Bailey's Irish Cream

½ oz vodka

½ oz butterscotch schnapps

½ oz pineapple juice

Stir ingredients with ice and strain into a chilled shot glass.

## RATTLESNAKE

1 oz Kahlúa

1 oz white crème de cacao

1 oz Bailey's Irish Cream

Layer the ingredients in the order listed in a cordial glass.

*Pickleback*

*Screaming Orgasm*

## REDHEADED SLUT

1 oz Jägermeister
1 oz peach schnapps
2 oz cranberry juice

Shake ingredients with ice and strain into a chilled cordial glass.

## RUSSIAN QUAALADE

1 oz Frangelico
1 oz Bailey's Irish Cream
1 oz vodka

Layer the ingredients in the order listed in a cordial glass.

## SCREAMING ORGASM

¼ oz vodka
¼ oz amaretto
¼ oz Bailey's Irish Cream
¼ oz Kahlúa

Shake ingredients with ice and strain into a chilled shot glass.

## RED SNAPPER

1 oz Canadian whisky
1 oz amaretto
2 oz cranberry juice

Shake ingredients with ice and strain into a chilled shot glass.

## SAMBUCA SLIDE

1 oz Sambuca
½ oz vodka
½ oz light cream

Stir ingredients with ice and strain into a chilled shot glass.

## SEX ON THE BEACH SHOOTER

½ oz black raspberry liqueur
½ oz Midori melon liqueur
½ oz vodka
1 oz pineapple juice
Cranberry juice

Stir all ingredients but the cranberry juice with ice and strain into a chilled cordial glass. Fill with cranberry juice.

## ROCKY MOUNTAIN

1 oz Tennessee whiskey
1 oz amaretto
½ oz lime juice

Shake ingredients with ice and strain into a chilled shot glass.

## SCOOTER

1 oz amaretto
1 oz brandy
1 oz light cream

Shake ingredients with ice and strain into a chilled cordial glass.

## SHAVETAIL

1 ½ oz peppermint schnapps
1 oz pineapple juice
1 oz light cream

Shake ingredients with ice and strain into a chilled cordial glass.

## SILVER SPIDER

½ oz vodka

½ oz rum

½ oz triple sec

½ oz white crème de menthe

Stir ingredients with ice and strain into a chilled shot glass.

## SNOWSHOE

¾ oz Wild Turkey bourbon whiskey

¾ oz peppermint schnapps

Shake ingredients with ice and strain into a chilled shot glass.

## SUITCASE

1 ½ oz bourbon

1 ½ oz lime cordial

Pour a shot each of bourbon and lime cordial. The lime cordial is to be drunk first and held in the mouth. Then the shot of bourbon is to be drunk, and the two liquids combined in the mouth.

## SLIPPERY NIPPLE

1 oz Bailey's Irish Cream

½ oz Sambuca

In a shot glass, float the Sambuca on the Bailey's.

## SOUR APPLE

¼ oz vodka

¼ oz apple liqueur

½ oz Midori melon liqueur

½ oz lemon-lime soda

Shake ingredients with ice and strain into a chilled shot glass.

## TEQUILA SHOT

1 ½ oz tequila

Lime wedge

Salt

Pour the tequila into a shot glass. The drinker should moisten the back of his or her hand between the base of the thumb and forefinger and sprinkle salt there. The sequence is to lick salt off the hand, drink the shot, and bite into the lime wedge as a chaser.

## SNAKEBITE

2 oz Yukon Jack Canadian whisky

½ oz preserved lime juice

Shake ingredients with ice and strain into a chilled shot glass.

## STALACTITE

1 ¼ oz Sambuca

¼ oz Bailey's Irish Cream

¼ oz black raspberry liqueur

In a cordial glass, float the Bailey's on the Sambuca. Then slowly drip in the raspberry liqueur.

## TEQUILA SLAMMER

1 oz tequila

1 oz lemon-lime soda

Combine the ingredients in a shot glass. The drinker should cover the glass with a napkin and the palm of one hand, slam the glass on the bar or table to agitate the ingredients, and drink immediately.

Stalactite

Tequila Slammer

### TERMINATOR

½ oz Kahlúa
½ oz Bailey's Irish Cream
½ oz Sambuca
½ oz Mandarine Napoléon
½ oz vodka

Layer the ingredients in a cordial glass in the order listed, from the bottom up.

### TO THE MOON

½ oz Kahlúa
½ oz amaretto
½ oz Bailey's Irish Cream
½ oz overproof rum

Stir ingredients with ice and strain into a chilled shot glass.

### WASHINGTON APPLE

1 oz Canadian whisky
1 oz sour apple schnapps
1 oz cranberry schnapps

Shake ingredients with ice and strain into a cordial glass. Garnish with a green apple slice if desired.

### THREE WISE MEN

½ oz Johnnie Walker Scotch whisky
½ oz Jack Daniel's Tennessee whiskey
½ oz Jim Beam bourbon whiskey

Shake ingredients with ice and strain into a chilled shot glass.

### TRAFFIC LIGHT

½ oz Midori melon liqueur
½ oz Galliano
½ oz crème de noyaux

Layer the ingredients in a cordial glass in the order listed, from the bottom up.

### WOO WOO

½ oz peach schnapps
½ oz vodka
1 oz cranberry juice

Shake ingredients with ice and strain into a chilled shot glass.

### TOASTIE SHOOTER

1 ½ oz amaretto
½ oz cinnamon schnapps

Combine ingredients in a shot glass.

*Three Wise Men*

*Woo Woo*

# SEASONAL DRINKS

Though most cocktails inhabit the perpetual season known as cocktail hour, many capture—or help create—the distinct mood of each quarter of the year.

## SPRING AND SUMMER

Light, refreshing cocktails dominate the spring. Consider such classics as slings, smashes, lemonade drinks, and colorful coolers. Go-to cocktail: a French 75. Summer is, of course, the season for clear and tropical cocktails. Fresh fruit fills the market stands, the sun pours down through long days, and a cold, sweet-and-tart drink is what you crave. While you could always go for a Gin and Tonic, for a bit more personality try one of the great Caribbean drinks—a classic Daiquiri will keep you cool.

## FALL AND WINTER

As Keats put it, autumn is the "season of mists and mellow fruitfulness," and that vibe is what you'll want in a cocktail. Deeper, richer drinks come to the fore. Any drink involving apple juice or apple brandy chimes with sentimental visions of autumn. Go-to cocktail: a Sidecar. When winter comes, linger over an Irish Coffee or Hot Toddy; or brace yourself against the cold with a potent whiskey drink—stay toasty warm with an Old Fashioned.

Whisky Daisy

Hot Cinnamon Roll

# HOT AND FROZEN
# DRINKS

HOT COCKTAILS HAVE A LONG HISTORY, HAVING BEEN
USED FOR CENTURIES TO WARM CHILLED TRAVELERS
AND BAR CUSTOMERS. FROZEN COCKTAILS ARE A MORE
RECENT DEVELOPMENT, BUT THEY OFFER A BRACING
KIND OF REFRESHMENT THAT IS PERFECT FOR STEAMY
SUMMER EVENINGS.

## ADULT HOT CHOCOLATE

1 ½ oz peppermint schnapps

6 oz hot chocolate

Whipped cream

Combine schnapps and hot chocolate in a mug and top with whipped cream.

## AMERICAN GROG

1 ½ oz light rum

¾ oz lemon juice

1 cube/tsp sugar

Hot water

Put the sugar cube in an Irish coffee glass and pour the lemon juice and rum over it. Fill with hot water.

## BOSTON CARIBBEAN COFFEE

1 oz dark crème de cacao

1 oz dark rum

Hot coffee

Whipped cream

Pour crème de cacao and rum into an Irish coffee glass and top with coffee and whipped cream.

## ALMOND CHOCOLATE KISS

1 oz amaretto

1 oz chocolate liqueur

5 oz hot chocolate

Stir ingredients in a warm mug.

## BISHOP

1 750ml bottle dry red wine

1 cinnamon stick

3 cloves

½ cup sugar

4 whole oranges

Roast the oranges in a 350° oven until brown, about 15 minutes. Place in a stockpot and add the sugar, spices, and half the wine and let macerate for a few hours. Then mash the fruit, add the rest of the wine, heat up, and serve in mugs or punch cups.

## CAFÉ L'ORANGE

½ oz Cognac

½ oz triple sec

1 oz Mandarine Napoléon

4 oz hot coffee

Whipped cream

Pour Cognac and liqueurs in an Irish coffee glass and top with coffee and whipped cream.

## AMARETTO TEA

2 oz amaretto

6 oz hot tea

Whipped cream

Pour hot tea into a warmed parfait glass. Top with amaretto and whipped cream.

## BLACK GOLD

¼ oz triple sec

¼ oz amaretto

¼ oz Bailey's Irish Cream

¼ oz Frangelico

4 oz hot coffee

Pour liqueurs into an Irish coffee glass and top with coffee, and add a dash of cinnamon schnapps if desired. Can be topped with whipped cream.

## CAFFÈ AMARETTO

1 oz amaretto

1 cup hot coffee

Whipped cream

Stir amaretto and coffee in an Irish coffee glass and top with whipped cream.

Caffè Amaretto

## CAPRICCIO

1 oz amaretto

½ oz brandy

½ oz crème de menthe

1 tsp sugar

Cinnamon sugar, for rimming glass

Hot coffee

Whipped cream

Rim an Irish coffee glass with the cinnamon sugar. Pour the white sugar in the bottom of the glass and add the brandy and liqueurs. Fill with hot coffee and top with whipped cream.

## DOUBLEMINT

1 oz spearmint schapps

Dash of green crème de menthe

Hot coffee

Whipped cream

Pour schnapps in an Irish coffee glass and fill with coffee. Top with whipped cream and drizzle on green crème de menthe.

## HOT BRANDY ALEXANDER

¾ oz brandy

¾ oz crème de cacao

4 oz steamed milk

Combine ingredients in an Irish coffee glass. Can be topped with whipped cream if desired.

## CHOCOLATE COFFEE KISS

¾ oz Kahlúa

¾ oz Bailey's Irish Cream

Splash of dark crème de cacao

Splash of Mandarine Napoléon

1 ½ oz chocolate syrup

Hot coffee

Whipped cream

Combine first five ingredients in an Irish coffee glass and fill with coffee. Top with whipped cream.

## GROG

1 ½ oz dark rum

1 oz honey syrup (equal parts honey and warm water, mixed and then chilled)

¾ oz lemon juice

4 oz hot water or black tea

1 cinnamon stick

Combine all ingredients in a mug and stir.

## HOT BRANDY TODDY

2 oz brandy

1 cube/tsp sugar

Hot water or black tea

Lemon slice

Put sugar in the bottom of an Irish coffee glass and fill 2/3 full with hot water or tea. Add brandy and stir. Garnish with lemon slice.

## COFFEE NUDGE

½ oz brandy

½ oz Kahlúa

½ oz dark crème de cacao

Hot coffee

Whipped cream

In an Irish coffee glass, combine the first three ingredients. Fill with coffee and top with whipped cream.

## HOT APPLE PIE

2 oz Tuaca citrus liqueur

6 oz hot apple cider

Whipped cream

Pour Tuaca in an Irish coffee glass and fill with hot cider. Top with whipped cream if desired.

## HOT BUTTERED RUM

2 oz dark rum

1 tsp brown sugar

1 tbsp butter

Hot water or tea

Put sugar in the bottom of an Irish coffee glass and fill 2/3 full with hot water or tea. Add rum and stir.

Hot Brandy Alexander

Grog

Hot Brandy Toddy

## HOT CINNAMON ROLL

1 ½ oz cinnamon schnapps

Hot apple cider

Whipped cream

Combine cider and schnapps in an Irish coffee glass. Top with whipped cream if desired.

## HOT GIN TODDY

1 oz gin

1 tbsp honey

¼ lemon

1 cup hot tea

Pour the honey in an Irish coffee glass. Add the gin and the squeezed juice of the lemon quarter and top with the tea.

## HOT KISS

½ oz white crème de menthe

½ oz white crème de cacao

1 oz Irish whiskey

6 oz hot coffee

Whipped cream

Pour liqueurs and whiskey into an Irish coffee glass and add coffee. Top with whipped cream.

## HOT RUM TODDY

1 oz rum

1 tbsp honey

¼ lemon

1 cup hot tea

Pour the honey in an Irish coffee glass. Add the rum and the squeezed juice of the lemon quarter and top with the tea.

## HOT SHOT

½ oz Galliano

½ oz espresso

½ oz heavy cream

Layer the ingredients in ascending order in a shot glass.

## HOT WHISKEY TODDY

1 oz whiskey of choice

1 tbsp honey

¼ lemon

1 cup hot tea

Pour the honey in an Irish coffee glass. Add the whiskey and the squeezed juice of the lemon quarter and top with the tea.

## IRISH COFFEE

1 ½ oz Irish whiskey

Hot coffee

Whipped cream

Pour the whiskey in an Irish coffee glass and fill with coffee. Add sugar if desired, and top with whipped cream.

## ITALIAN COFFEE

½ oz amaretto

Hot coffee

1 oz coffee ice cream

Pour amaretto into an Irish coffee glass and nearly fill with coffee. Top with ice cream.

## JAMAICA COFFEE

1 oz coffee brandy

¾ oz light or gold rum

Hot coffee

Whipped cream

Combine brandy and rum in an Irish coffee glass and fill with coffee. Top with whipped cream.

*Hot Whiskey Toddy*

*Irish Coffee*

## MEXICAN COFFEE

1 oz Kahlúa

½ oz tequila

Hot coffee

Whipped cream

Pour Kahlúa and tequila into an Irish coffee glass and fill with coffee. Top with whipped cream.

## NAVY GROG

1 ½ oz dark rum

1 oz orange Curaçao

¼ oz lime juice

2 oz water

2 oz orange juice

Dash of Angostura bitters

Combine ingredients in a saucepan and heat until warm. Serve in a mug.

## SPANISH COFFEE

1 oz Spanish brandy

Hot coffee

Whipped cream

Pour the brandy into an Irish coffee glass, fill with coffee, and top with whipped cream.

*Mexican Coffee*

*Spanish Coffee*

# COCKTAIL
## PARTY THEMES

Here are a few classic ideas for cocktail party themes—just add a good mix of friends.

### CASABLANCA

This theme has it all: Hollywood glamour, an exotic locale, romance, and drama. Set up a space like Rick's Café and serve champagne cocktails in a casino room. Whoever comes as Claude Rains's Captain Louis Renault gets priority at the bar.

### TROPICANA

Warm weather, an indoor/outdoor space, a pool or beach if available, exotic flowers and tiki torches, and plenty of tropical cocktails.

### SPEAKEASY

Hand out party pearls, feather boas, and fans to women in flapper dresses and men in dark suits (or pastel suits, if they want to get Gatsbyesque). Play period jazz and serve gin-based drinks.

### GARDEN PARTY

In classic English style, serve up Pimm's punch and G and T (Gin and Tonic) while inviting guests to stroll through the garden and play outdoor games. Men can wear blazers and boater hats; women, pastel dresses and Ascot-style hats.

*Gin and Tonic*

*Pimms and Lemonade*

## APPLE COLADA

2 oz apple schnapps

1 oz cream of coconut

1 oz half-and-half

Apple slice

Maraschino cherry

Combine the first three ingredients with crushed ice in a blender and blend until smooth. Pour into a highball or other tall glass and garnish with apple slice and cherry.

## APPLE RIVER INNER TUBE

1 oz brandy

1 oz dark crème de cacao

1 ½ scoops of vanilla ice cream

Apple slice, half ring

Combine all ingredients but apple with 1 cup of crushed ice in a blender and blend until smooth. Pour into a parfait glass and garnish with the apple slice.

## BANANA DI AMORE

1 oz amaretto

1 oz crème de banane

2 oz orange juice

1 oz simple syrup

½ oz lemon juice

Orange slice

Combine all ingredients but orange slice in a blender with 1 cup crushed ice and blend until smooth. Serve in a red wine glass and garnish with orange slice.

## APPLE GRANNY CRISP

1 oz apple schnapps

½ oz brandy

½ oz Bailey's Irish Cream

2 scoops of vanilla ice cream

Graham cracker crumbs

Whipped cream

Combine first four ingredients in a blender until smooth. Serve in a parfait glass topped with whipped cream and a sprinkling of cracker crumbs.

## BAY CITY BOMBER

½ oz vodka

½ oz tequila

½ oz gin

½ oz triple sec

1 oz orange juice

1 oz pineapple juice

1 oz cranberry juice

1 oz simple syrup

½ oz lemon juice

½ oz overproof rum

Combine all ingredients except rum in a blender with 1 cup crushed ice and blend until smooth. Pour into a parfait glass and top with a float of rum.

## BANANA DAIQUIRI

1 ½ oz light rum

½ oz triple sec

1 ½ oz lime juice

1 tsp sugar

Maraschino cherry

1 medium banana, sliced

Combine ingredients except cherry in a blender with 1 cup crushed ice and blend until smooth. Pour into a tall glass and garnish with cherry.

## BANANA FOSTER

1 ½ oz spiced rum

½ oz banana liqueur

2 scoops of vanilla ice cream

1 medium banana, sliced

Ground cinnamon

Combine ingredicnts except cinnamon in a blender with 1 cup crushed ice and blend until smooth. Pour into a large brandy snifter and dust with cinnamon.

*Apple Colada*

*Banana Daiquiri*

## BIG CHILL

1 ½ oz dark rum

1 oz pineapple juice

1 oz orange juice

1 oz cranberry juice

1 oz cream of coconut

Pineapple wedge

Maraschino cherry

Combine ingredients except fruits in a blender with 1 cup crushed ice and blend until smooth. Pour into a tall glass and garnish with pineapple wedge and cherry.

## BLIZZARD

1 oz brandy

1 oz Bailey's Irish Cream

1 oz Kahlúa

1 oz light rum

2 scoops of vanilla ice cream

Splash of light cream

Ground nutmeg

Combine all ingredients but nutmeg in a blender and blend until smooth. Pour into a large brandy snifter and dust with nutmeg.

## BLUE VELVET

1 oz black raspberry liqueur

1 oz Midori

4 oz vanilla ice cream

Whipped cream

Dash of Blue Curaçao

Combine liqueurs (except Blue Caraçao) and ice cream in a blender with 1 cup crushed ice and blend until smooth. Pour into a parfait glass, top with whipped cream, and drizzle Blue Curaçao on top.

## BLUSHIN' RUSSIAN

1 oz Kahlúa

¾ oz vodka

1 scoop of vanilla ice cream

4 fresh strawberries

Chocolate-dipped strawberry

Combine Kahlúa, vodka, ice cream, and strawberries in a blender and blend until smooth. Pour into a parfait glass and garnish with dipped strawberry.

## BRASS FIDDLE

2 oz peach schnapps

¾ oz Tennessee whiskey

2 oz pineapple juice

1 oz orange juice

1 oz grenadine syrup

Pineapple wedge

Maraschino cherry

Combine schnapps, whiskey, and juices in a blender with 1 cup ice and blend until smooth. Swirl the grenadine in a parfait glass and add the blended ingredients. Garnish with pineapple wedge and cherry.

## CANYON QUAKE

¾ oz Bailey's Irish Cream

¾ oz brandy

1 oz amaretto

2 oz light cream

Combine ingredients in a blender with 1 cup crushed ice and blend until smooth. Pour into a large brandy snifter.

## CHAMPAGNE CORNUCOPIA

1 oz vodka

¾ oz peach schnapps

1 oz champagne

1 oz cranberry juice

2 scoops of rainbow sherbet

Orange slice

Combine sherbet, vodka, and schnapps in a blender and blend until smooth. Pour cranberry juice in a large red wine glass and top with the blended ingredients, pouring in a spiral pattern. Top with a float of champagne and garnish with orange slice.

## CHILLY IRISHMAN

1 oz Irish whiskey

½ oz Kahlúa

½ oz Bailey's Irish Cream

3 oz espresso, chilled

Dash of simple syrup

1 scoop of vanilla ice cream

Combine ingredients in a blender with 4 cups crushed ice and blend until smooth. Serve in parfait glasses.

*Canyon Quake*

*Chilly Irishman*

## CHOCOLATE ALMOND CREAM

4 oz amaretto

4 oz white crème de cacao

1 qt vanilla ice cream

Chocolate shavings

Combine ingredients except chocolate shavings in a blender and blend until smooth. Pour into parfait glasses and garnish with chocolate shavings.

## CHOCOLATE CHAOS

1 ½ oz chocolate vodka

½ oz dark crème de cacao

2 oz chocolate syrup

1 scoop of chocolate ice cream

Whipped cream

Combine first four ingredients in a blender with ½ cup crushed ice and blend until smooth. Serve in a parfait glass topped with whipped cream.

## CLOUD NINE

1 oz Bailey's Irish Cream

½ oz black raspberry liqueur

1 oz amaretto

1 scoop of vanilla ice cream

Whipped cream

1 Reese's peanut butter cup

Combine the liqueurs and ice cream in a blender and blend until smooth. Pour into a parfait glass, top with the whipped cream, and garnish with the peanut butter cup.

## CHOCOLATE BANANA COLADA

2 oz light rum

1 oz chocolate liqueur

½ oz dark crème de cacao

½ oz banana liqueur

½ oz cream of coconut

1 medium banana, sliced

Combine ingredients in a blender with 1 cup crushed ice and blend until smooth. Serve in a parfait glass.

## CHOCOLATE COCONUT CREAM PIE

1 oz Malibu

1 oz Bailey's Irish Cream

½ oz Kahlúa

1 tbsp shredded coconut

1 scoop of chocolate ice cream

Combine ingredients in a blender with ½ cup crushed ice and blend until smooth. Serve in a parfait glass.

## DEATH BY CHOCOLATE

1 oz Bailey's Irish Cream

½ oz dark crème de cacao

½ oz vodka

1 scoop of chocolate ice cream

Whipped cream

Chocolate shavings

Combine first four ingredients in a blender with 1 cup crushed ice and blend until smooth. Pour into a parfait glass and garnish with whipped cream and chocolate shavings.

## FROZEN CHOCOLATE BANANA SMASH

1 ½ oz Bailey's Irish Cream

¼ oz vanilla extract

½ oz light cream

½ scoop of vanilla ice cream

½ banana, sliced

Whipped cream

Combine first five ingredients in a blender with 1 cup crushed ice and blend until smooth. Top with whipped cream.

## CHOCOLATE COLADA

2 oz rum

1 oz cream of coconut

1 oz chocolate syrup

Dash of light cream

Combine ingredients in a blender with ½ cup crushed ice and blend until smooth. Serve in a parfait glass.

## DEVIL'S TAIL

1 ½ oz light rum

1 oz vodka

¾ oz apricot brandy

½ oz lime juice

¾ oz grenadine syrup

Combine ingredients in a blender with 1 cup crushed ice and blend until smooth. Pour into a champagne flute.

*Devil's Tail*

### DI AMORE DREAM

1 ½ oz Amaretto di Amore

¾ oz white crème de cacao

2 oz orange juice

2 scoops of vanilla ice cream

Orange slice

Combine all ingredients but orange slice in a blender with 1 cup crushed ice and blend until smooth. Pour into a parfait glass. Garnish with orange slice.

### FROZEN BERKELEY

1 ½ oz light rum

½ oz brandy

½ oz passion fruit nectar

½ oz lemon juice

Combine ingredients in a blender with 1 cup crushed ice and blend until smooth. Pour into a champagne flute.

### FROZEN CHI CHI

2 oz vodka

½ oz Blue Curaçao

½ oz cream of coconut

½ cup fresh or canned pineapple

1 scoop of vanilla ice cream

Pineapple wedge

Combine all ingredients except pineapple wedge in a blender with ½ cup crushed ice and blend until smooth. Pour into a parfait glass and garnish with pineapple wedge.

### DREAMY MONKEY

1 oz vodka

½ oz crème de banane

½ oz dark crème de cacao

1 banana

2 scoops of vanilla ice cream

1 oz light cream

Whipped cream

Combine all ingredients but whipped cream in a blender and blend until smooth, reserving half the banana. Pour in a parfait glass, top with whipped cream, and garnish with reserved banana half.

### FROZEN BLUE HAWAIIAN

2 oz vodka

Splash of Blue Curaçao

4 oz pineapple juice

1 ½ oz lemon juice

1 oz simple syrup

Combine ingredients in a blender with ½ cup crushed ice and blend until smooth. Pour into a parfait glass.

### FROZEN DAIQUIRI

2 oz light rum

1 ½ oz lime juice

¾ oz simple syrup

Lime wedge

Combine all ingredients but lime wedge in a blender with 1 cup crushed ice and blend until smooth. Pour into a chilled Collins glass and garnish with lime wedge.

### FROSTY NOGGIN

1 ½ oz rum

¾ oz white crème de menthe

Dash of green crème de menthe

3 oz eggnog

2 scoops of vanilla ice cream

Whipped cream

Combine all ingredients but whipped cream in a blender and blend until smooth. Pour into a parfait glass and top with whipped cream.

### FROZEN CAPPUCCINO

½ oz Bailey's Irish Cream

½ oz Kahlúa

½ oz Frangelico

1 scoop of vanilla ice cream

Dash of light cream

Combine ingredients in a blender with 1 cup crushed ice and blend until smooth. Pour into a parfait glass.

### FROZEN FUZZY

1 oz peach schnapps

½ oz triple sec

½ oz lime juice

½ oz grenadine syrup

Splash of lemon-lime soda

Combine ingredients in a blender with 1 cup crushed ice and blend until smooth. Pour into a champagne flute.

Frozzen Blue Hawaiian

## FROZEN MARGARITA

1 ½ oz tequila

½ oz triple sec

1 oz lime juice

Lime slice

Combine ingredients except lime slice in a blender with 1 cup crushed ice and blend until smooth. Pour into a cocktail glass and garnish with lime slice.

## GULF STREAM

1 oz Blue Curaçao

3 oz champagne

½ oz light rum

½ oz brandy

6 oz lemonade

1 oz lime juice

Combine ingredients in a blender with 1 cup crushed ice and blend until smooth. Pour into a parfait glass.

## ITALIAN DREAM

1 ½ oz Bailey's Irish Cream

½ oz amaretto

2 oz light cream

Combine ingredients in a blender with 1 cup crushed ice and blend until smooth. Pour into a parfait glass.

## FROZEN PINEAPPLE DAIQUIRI

1 ½ oz light rum

4 pineapple chunks

½ oz lime juice

Dash of sugar

Combine ingredients in a blender with 1 cup crushed ice and blend until smooth. Pour into a champagne flute.

## ICED COFFEE À L'ORANGE

8 oz triple sec

1 qt vanilla ice cream

4 tsp instant coffee

Orange slices

Combine first three ingredients in a blender and blend until smooth. Pour into parfait glasses and garnish with orange slices.

## JAMAICAN BANANA

½ oz light rum

½ oz white crème de cacao

½ oz crème de banane

2 of scoops vanilla ice cream

1 oz half-and-half

1 banana

Ground nutmeg

Combine ingredients except nutmeg in a blender with 1 cup crushed ice and blend until smooth. Pour into a large brandy snifter and dust with nutmeg.

## FROZEN STRAWBERRY DAIQUIRI

2 oz light rum

½ oz triple sec

1 oz lime juice

½ tsp sugar

Several strawberries

Combine ingredients in a blender with 1 cup crushed ice and blend until smooth. Pour into a Collins glass.

## IRISH DREAM

½ oz Bailey's Irish Cream

½ oz Frangelico

¾ oz dark crème de cacao

4 oz vanilla ice cream

Whipped cream

Combine all ingredients but whipped cream in a blender with 1 cup crushed ice and blend until smooth. Pour into pint glasses and top with whipped cream.

## KOKOMO JOE

1 oz light rum

1 oz banana liqueur

5 oz orange juice

2 oz pineapple juice

1 oz cream of coconut

½ banana

Orange slice

Combine all ingredients but orange slice in a blender with 1 cup crushed ice and blend until smooth. Pour into a parfait glass and garnish with orange slice.

*Frozen Margarita*

*Frozen Strawberry Daiquiri*

*Irish Dream*

*Kokomo Joe*

## MAUI BREEZE

½ oz amaretto

½ oz triple sec

½ oz brandy

1 oz simple syrup

½ oz lemon juice

2 oz orange juice

2 oz guava juice

Orchid

Combine all ingredients but the orchid in a blender with 1 cup crushed ice and blend until smooth. Pour into a parfait glass and garnish with the orchid.

## NUTTY COLADA

3 oz amaretto

1 ½ oz coconut milk

1 ½ oz crushed pineapple

Combine ingredients in a blender with 1 cup crushed ice and blend until smooth. Pour into a Collins glass.

## OVER THE RAINBOW

2 oz spiced rum

1 oz orange curaçao

2 scoops of rainbow sherbet

4 peach slices, peeled

2 strawberries

Combine ingredients in a blender with 1 cup crushed ice, reserving one strawberry and peach slice. Blend until smooth. Pour into a parfait glass and garnish with reserved fruit.

## PEACH MELBA FREEZE

¾ oz peach schnapps

¾ oz black raspberry liqueur

¾ oz Frangelico

1 scoop of vanilla ice cream

¾ oz light cream

1 oz raspberry jam

Peach slice

Combine all ingredients but peach slice in a blender and blend until smooth. Pour into a parfait glass and garnish with peach slice.

## PEACHY AMARETTO

8 oz amaretto

1 cup canned peaches

2 scoops of vanilla ice cream

Combine ingredients in a blender and blend until smooth. Pour into a parfait glass.

## PEPPERMINT PENGUIN

½ oz green crème de menthe

½ oz chocolate mint liqueur

4 chocolate sandwich cookies

3 oz light cream

Whipped cream

Combine ingredients in a blender with 1 cup crushed ice, reserving one cookie and the whipped cream. Blend until smooth. Pour into a parfait glass, top with whipped cream, and garnish with reserved cookie.

## RASPBERRY CHEESECAKE

1 oz white crème de cacao

1 oz black raspberry liqueur

½ oz / 1 tbsp cream cheese, softened

2 scoops of vanilla ice cream

Combine ingredients in a blender with 1 cup crushed ice and blend until smooth. Pour into a parfait glass.

## STRAWBERRIES AND CREAM

1 oz strawberry schnapps

1 ½ tbsp sugar

2 oz half-and-half

2 strawberries

Combine schnapps, sugar, and half-and-half in a blender and blend until smooth. Add strawberries and blend for a few seconds more. Pour into a parfait glass.

## STRAWBERRY SHORTCAKE

1 oz amaretto

¾ oz white crème de cacao

3 oz strawberries in syrup

1 scoop of vanilla ice cream

Whipped cream

1 fresh strawberry

Combine all ingredients but the whipped cream and strawberry in a blender and blend until smooth. Pour into a large red wine glass, top with whipped cream, and garnish with fresh strawberry.

*Strawberry Shortcake*

### TENNESSEE WALTZ

1 ¼ oz peach schnapps

2 oz pineapple juice

1 oz passion fruit nectar

1 scoop of vanilla ice cream

Whipped cream

Fresh strawberry

Combine all ingredients but the strawberry and whipped cream in a blender and blend until smooth. Pour into a parfait glass, top with whipped cream, and garnish with strawberry

### TEQUILA FROST

1 ¼ oz tequila

1 ¼ oz pineapple juice

1 ¼ oz grapefruit juice

½ oz honey

½ oz grenadine syrup

2 oz vanilla ice cream

Orange slice

Combine all ingredients but the orange slice in a blender and blend until smooth. Pour into a parfait glass and garnish with the orange slice.

### TROLLEY CAR

1 ¼ oz amaretto

6 fresh strawberries

2 scoops of vanilla ice cream

Combine ingredients in a blender and blend until smooth, reserving one strawberry. Pour into a parfait glass and garnish with the reserved strawberry.

*Tequila Frost*

*Trolley Car*

# CHAMPAGNE COCKTAILS

Champagne cocktails occupy a distinct niche in cocktail culture. At once colorful and elegant, festive and intimate, they lend themselves not only to romantic settings but also to expansive parties. While a Kir Royale may be a glamorous and inviting nightcap, it's not unusual to have a Mimosa with brunch the next day. Here are a few delicious recipes to keep in mind.

## ALPHONSO COCKTAIL

1 sugar cube soaked in Angostura bitters

1 oz Red Dubonnet

Champagne

Lemon peel

Place sugar cube in a white wine glass with two or three ice cubes. Add Dubonnet, then fill with champagne. Garnish with lemon peel.

## BELLINI

1 ½ oz peach puree

3 oz Prosecco or other dry sparkling wine

½ oz peach liqueur

Pour the peach puree in the bottom of a mixing glass. Gently pour in and blend the Prosecco. Strain mixture into a champagne flute. Float peach liqueur on top.

## CLASSIC CHAMPAGNE COCKTAIL

Champagne

Sugar cube soaked in Angostura bitters

Lemon peel

Place the sugar cube in the bottom of a champagne flute. Slowly fill with the champagne. Garnish with lemon peel if desired.

### KIR ROYALE

¼ oz Cassis or Framboise liqueur

Champagne

Lemon peel

Pour the Cassis or Framboise into a champagne flute. Fill with champagne. Garnish with lemon peel if desired.

### MIMOSA

4 oz champagne

2 oz fresh orange juice

Pour the orange juice into a champagne flute and fill with champagne.

### POINSETTIA

2 oz cranberry juice

4 oz champagne

½ oz Cointreau or triple sec

Pour cranberry juice into a champagne flute. Fill with champagne. Top with a float of Cointreau or triple sec.

# INDEX OF COCKTAILS BY BASE LIQUOR

What follows is a guide for locating drinks by their base liquors—that is, the liquor that takes up the most volume in the drink or, in a looser sense, defines the drink's character. In some cases, such as that of Long Island Iced Tea, the combination of liquors is so evenly spread that I have simply chosen one by which to list it here. In other cocktails, especially those that include liqueurs, an ingredient that may not be the base liquor in terms of volume may still dominate the drink; those I have listed under the dominant liquor. Of course, these are subjective judgments, but they should more or less hold true for most palates. With that principle in mind, I have not individually listed the hundreds of variations on the martini and the margarita; though some of those drinks diverge from the norm, most use the same base alcohols and present relatively modest variations on a common theme. Finally, some of the drinks are listed as appearing on two pages, with a slash between; this indicates two slightly different ways of preparing or presenting the drink.

## BRANDY DRINKS

Technically, brandy is a spirit distilled from wine, but that doesn't mean that all brandy comes from grapes. Spirits under this category range from Cognac and Armagnac to apple brandy (applejack, or in some cases Calvados), apricot brandy, and even pisco, among others. Of course, it wouldn't do at all to use a 1988 Hine Cognac in a mixed drink—choose something more modest for your cocktail bar.

## GIN DRINKS

It's worth noting that, like most alcoholic beverages, gin is more complex and varied than one might think; it's not simply a clear, juniper-flavored spirit. When someone refers to gin, they usually mean the benchmark style: London dry gin. But one can also find the fuller and more aromatic Plymouth gin, the sweeter, old-fashioned Old Tom gin, and of course sloe gin, which is reddish in color and infused with blackthorn fruit. The recent revival of cocktail culture has led to a rise in boutique gins, some of which barely qualify as gin at all, but many of which are delicious.

## LIQUEURS AND SCHNAPPS

While these two categories fit together only loosely—most schnapps are significantly stronger than most liqueurs—what they have in common is powerful flavors, usually of infused herbs, berries, and other botanicals. Be careful mixing drinks with liqueurs and schnapps; if not carefully balanced with other ingredients, many of them can severely distort the flavor of a cocktail.

## RUM AND CACHAÇA DRINKS

Rum, originally a by-product of the sugar trade and then a mainstay of the British navy, has been popular in America since colonial times. In recent years, distillers have begun to market increasingly complex and sophisticated rums, and boutique distilleries have found enthusiastic drinkers. In mixing cocktails, it's important to distinguish among light, gold, and dark rums, which have very different characters as a result of barrel aging and other variables. Cachaça, the sugarcane-derived spirit whose home is Brazil, is a close relative of rum. As with brandy, don't waste your top-shelf sipping rum on a mixed drink.

## TEQUILA DRINKS

Tequila, which is distilled from the agave plant, is thousands of years old and comes in a range of styles, from the light and often crude silver to the aged and sophisticated añejo. Given that, for many years, only relatively cheap varieties were available in America, tequila has long suffered from a somewhat justified reputation as a particularly unforgiving spirit. Recently, however, its more elegant and complex expressions have begun finding their way to American shelves. As with some other spirits, don't use your fine añejo in a mixed drink—silver or gold tequila will do just fine.

## VODKA DRINKS

Vodka is the most popular spirit for mixing drinks. This is mainly because, as a rectified spirit that is filtered many times, it is the most neutral base alcohol at any bar and thus allows other cocktail ingredients to come to the fore. As with other spirits, vodka has benefitted from a boom in boutique and upscale brands. While much of this is just clever marketing, there are differences in quality (in every sense of that word), and they're worth exploring. Also, the variety of infused vodkas has made for a remarkable array of interesting cocktail recipes.

# WHISKEY DRINKS

There are no doubt purists who are outraged to see the various kinds of whiskey lumped together under one heading. And they have a point: whiskeys are made from different grains, in different settings, in a range of styles. For starters, Scotch is very different from bourbon, and further differences separate Irish, Canadian, Japanese, and even Indian whiskies, to say nothing of rye. But when it comes to mixing cocktails, there is a common denominator to the flavor profiles of all whiskeys, and their distinct expressions tend to be variations on that theme. Again, there is no sense in using exceptional whiskey for a mixed drink. Use good Campbeltown Scotch for a sour drink, and you'll not only have wasted a fine sipping beverage; you'll have done injury to the soul of Scotland.

## WINE AND FORTIFIED WINES

Cocktails made from wine and fortified wines have a long and rich history, dating back to the mulled wines of ancient times and the fortified punches so often associated with 18th-century England and America. Their flavors range from the most hearty to the most refined. As with other mixed drinks, don't use the good stuff—vintage Pol Roger should not go into Poinsettias.

## NON-ALCOHOLIC DRINKS

Every bar, at home or elsewhere, should include non-alcoholic drinks. Some, such as sangrita, serve as ingredients in traditional cocktails but can also be enjoyed on their own. And the best thing is, you can drink as much as you like.

# ACKNOWLEDGMENTS

Special thanks to Jeremy Baile at RGB Digital for
the creation of many of the special photographs
in this book. www.rgbdigital.co.uk

2-3 RGB Digital • 4l Shutterstock/ bogdanhoda • 4r Shutterstock/Igor Klimov • 5 Shutterstock/bogdanhoda •
6-7 Shutterstock/bogdanhoda • 8 RGB Digital • 11 RGB Digital • 12 RGB Digital • 15 RGB Digital • 16
Shutterstock/Shebeko • 19 RGB Digital • 21t Shutterstock/Nastya22 • 21b Shutterstock/Wallertz • 22 RGB Digital
• 23 RGB Digital • 25 RGB Digital • 27 RGB Digital • 29 RGB Digital • 30 RGB Digital • 31 Shutterstock/
Dream79 • 33 RGB Digital • 34 RGB Digital/Philippa Baile • 35 RGB Digital • 37 RGB Digital/Philippa Baile
• 39 Shutterstock/NDT • 41 RGB Digital/Philippa Baile • 43 RGB Digital • 44 RGB Digital/Philippa Baile • 45
Shutterstock/Nataliya Hora • 47 Shutterstock/3523studio • 49 Shutterstock/Serhiy Shullye • 51 Shutterstock/
MSPhotographic • 53 Shutterstock/Bochkarev Photography • 54 Shutterstock/Loskutnikov • 55t Shutterstock/
ENVY • 55b Shutterstock/Patty Orly • 56 Shutterstock/stockcreations • 57 RGB Digital • 59tl Shutterstock/Alexey
Lysenko • 59tr Shutterstock/KKnD • 58-59b RGB Digital • 60 RGB Digital • 62 RGB Digital • 63 RGB Digital •
64 RGB Digital • 65 RGB Digital • 66 Shutterstock/joannawnuk • 67 RGB Digital • 68 RGB Digital • 69 RGB
Digital • 71 Shutterstock/Palle Christensen • 73 Shutterstock/3523studio • 74 RGB Digital • 75 RGB Digital •
77 RGB Digital/Philippa Baile • 78tl RGB Digital • 78bl Shutterstock/nanka • 78r Shutterstock/StudioNewmarket
• 80 RGB Digital/Philippa Baile • 83t Shutterstock/gresei • 83b Shutterstock/Max Sugar 85l Shutterstock/Johan
Teodorsson • 85r Shutterstock/3523studio • 87tl Shutterstock/HG Photography • 87tr Shutterstock/Letizia Spanio
• 87b Shutterstock/gresei • 89 tl Shutterstock/3523studio • 89tr Shutterstock/Jag_cz • 89bl Shutterstock/verca
• 89br Shutterstock/Martin Turzak • 90l Shutterstock/Bochkarev Photography • 90tr Shutterstock/Wollertz • 90br
Shutterstock/stockcreations • 93 Shutterstock/Shebeko • 94 Shutterstock/Palmer Kane LLC • 95 Shutterstock/
Denis Vrublevski • 96 RGB Digital • 99 RGB Digital • 100 RGB Digital • 101 Shutterstock/Lidante • 103 RGB
Digital • 105 RGB Digital • 107 Shutterstock/svry • 108 RGB Digital/Philippa Baile • 109 RGB Digital/Philippa
Baile • 111 RGB Digital • 112 RGB Digital/Philippa Baile • 114 Shutterstock/gresei • 115 RGB Digital • 116
RGB Digital/Philippa Baile • 117 RGB Digital • 119 RGB Digital • 121 RGB Digital • 123 RGB Digital • 124 RGB
Digital • 125 RGB Digital • 126-127 RGB Digital • 127 tl Shutterstock/silver-john • 127tr Shutterstock/Roman
Sigaev • 128 RGB Digital • 131tl RGB Digital • 131bl Shutterstock/Lukaszewicz • 131tr Shutterstock/Wiktory •
131cr Shutterstock/Peter Kim • 131br Shutterstock/svry • 132 RGB Digital • 133 RGB Digital • 135 Shutterstock/
svry • 137 Shutterstock/svry • 139 RGB Digital • 140 Shutterstock/Max Sugar • 143t Shutterstock/Max Sugar •
143b Shutterstock/Wollertz • 145 RGB Digital • 147 RGB Digital • 148 RGB Digital • 149 RGB Digital • 150t
Shutterstock/White Room • 150b Shutterstock/Max Sugar • 153 RGB Digital • 155t Shutterstock/3523studio •
155b Shutterstock/martiapunts • 157t Shutterstock/Wollertz • 157b Shutterstock/3523studio • 158 Shutterstock/
Elizaveta Shagliy • 159 Shutterstock/martiapunts • 160 RGB Digital • 161 RGB Digital • 162 RGB Digital • 164-
165 Getty/Archive Photos • 165bl Shutterstock/Igor Normann • 165br Shutterstock/wavebreakmedia • 167 RGB
Digital/Philippa Baile • 169t Shutterstock/April Turner • 169b Shutterstock/Olaf Speier • 170 Shutterstock/John
Wollwerth • 173 Shutterstock/nikkytok • 174 RGB Digital/Philippa Baile • 177 Shutterstock/Nitr • 178 Shutterstock/
Aleksandra Zaitseva • 179 Shutterstock/Wollertz • 180 Shutterstock/Madlen • 181 Shutterstock/White Room • 182
Shutterstock/phloem • 183 Shutterstock/3523studio • 185t Shutterstock/Igor Normann • 185b Shutterstock/Sandra
Kemppainen • 186 Shutterstock/Alexander Sherstobitov • 189 Shutterstock/Dmitri Lobanov • 191 Shutterstock/
Wollertz • 193t Shutterstock/Karin Hildebrand Lau • 193b Shutterstock/3523studio • 195 Shutterstock/Wollertz •
197 RGB Digital • 199 RGB Digital • 201 RGB Digital • 202 RGB Digital/Philippa Baile • 205 RGB Digital/Philippa
Baile • 207t Shutterstock/Bochkarev Photography • 207b Shutterstock/Daniel Etzold • 209t Shutterstock/Cristi
Lucaci • 209b Shutterstock/Johan Swanepoel • 211 RGB Digital • 212 RGB Digital • 215 RGB Digital • 216 RGB
Digital • 219 RGB Digital • 221t Shutterstock/Ramon L. Farinos • 221b Shutterstock/Wollertz • 222 Shutterstock/
Africa Studio • 225 Shutterstock/Africa Studio • 226 Shutterstock/Bochkarev Photography • 227 Shutterstock/Petr
Jilek • 228-229 Getty/Carl Court • 229tl RGB Digital • 229tr Shutterstock/Palmer Kane LLC • 231 RGB Digital/
Philippa Baile • 233 RGB Digital/Philippa Baile • 234 RGB Digital • 237t RGB Digital • 237b RGB Digital • 239
RGB Digital/Philippa Baile • 240l Shutterstock/3523studio • 240r Shutterstock/White Room • 243t RGB Digital
• 243b RGB Digital • 245t Shutterstock/Palmer Kane LLC • 245c Shutterstock/Hitdelight • 245b Shutterstock/
Palle Christensen • 246 Shutterstock/ENVY • 249l Shutterstock/Wollertz • 249r Shutterstock/Andrew Thomas •
251 RGB Digital • 252 RGB Digital • 255 Shutterstock/3523studio • 256 Shutterstock/Wiktory • 259 RGB Digital
• 260 Shutterstock/Grant Terry • 263 Shutterstock/Wollertz • 265 Shutterstock/Maggee • 266 RGB Digital/Philippa
Baile • 269t RGB Digital/Philippa Baile • 269b Shutterstock/Alexander Pekour • 270t Shutterstock/Michael C. Gray
• 270b Shutterstock/Igor Normann • 273 RGB Digital • 275 RGB Digital • 276 RGB Digital • 279t Shutterstock/
Yeko Photo Studio • 279b Shutterstock/Mikhail Staroddubov • 280 Shutterstock/Lecic • 281 Shutterstock/Robert
Voight • 282-283 Shutterstock/Jay Ondreicka • 283tl Shutterstock/Christin Slavkov • 283tr Shutterstock/Lapina
Maria • 284 Shutterstock/Andriy Malakhovskyy • 287 Shutterstock/Lukaszewicz • 289tl Shutterstock/urbanlight •
289tr Shutterstock/Scaffer • 289b Shutterstock/Liv friis-larsen • 291l Shutterstock/AGfoto • 291r Shutterstock/
Scaffer • 292 Shutterstock/Vitaly Goncharov • 293 RGB Digital • 294-295 Shutterstock/Everett Collection • 295t
Shutterstock/MO_SES • 295b Shutterstock/Besjunior • 296 RGB Digital • 297 RGB Digital • 298 Shutterstock/
Dmitry Fischer • 299 RGB Digital • 301 RGB Digital/Philippa Baile • 303 RGB Digital • 305tl Shutterstock/
Cameron Whitman • 305tr Shutterstock/Scruggelgreen • 305bl Shutterstock/Settawat Udom • 305br Shutterstock/
Ignia Andrei • 307 Shutterstock/sutsaiy • 308 Shutterstock/Africa Studio • 309 Shutterstock/sutsaiy • 310-311
Shutterstock/Novoselov • 318 RGB Digital • 319 Shutterstock/Dan Peretz